DINING CUSTOMS AROUND THE WORLD

With Occasional Recipes

by

Alice Bonzi Mothershead

with illustrations by

Marilena Perrone

About the author...

Alice Bonzi Mothershead is now the Director of the Community Liaison
Center for Foreign Students and Americans Abroad of the Pasadena City
College. She has lived abroad and travelled extensively in Western
Europe, Africa, the Mediterranean area, Latin America, and Asia.

Her special interest in distinctive customs around the world was
reflected in a prior publication. Social Customs and Manners in the
United States: A Guide for Foreign Students. This publication was
so successful that proceeds from its sale were used to establish a
foreign student scholarship in the United States. Her observations,
while being entertained in homes abroad, and in-depth discussions
with foreign students and visitors while in the United States led to
the development of this book.

In addition to numerous professional honors within this country, she
was Knighted by the Republic of Italy in 1974.

ISBN 0-912048-29-8
LC   81-85930

Garrett Park Press
Garrett Park, Maryland 20896

TABLE OF CONTENTS

TABLE OF CONTENTS (Continued)

INTRODUCTION

This collection of cultural patterns is meant to be a brief guide for the curious--those persons who plan to live or travel abroad, those who assist students and visitors from other countries, those concerned in foods or cooking as a hobby, or those who are simply interested in social differences around the world.

Although this is not intended to be a cook book, occasional recipes or brief descriptions of foods have been included in order to explain more fully the nature of foods or customs in these geographical areas, or to offer an opportunity to experiment with a dish from another culture. The reason for these inclusions is also to demonstrate differences in habits and to thereby help the reader to recognize and understand the sometimes subtle and sometimes pronounced differences between the peoples of different lands. The many persons who contributed to the book almost always mentioned that their foods were good, that they missed their native cooking, or that they found it difficult at first to enjoy foreign cooking.

Many of the foods are described, rather than given as an exact recipe. Contributors rarely remembered the precise measurements but gave an idea of the ingredients to let the reader know the content of the mixtures. If you should wish to experiment with these loosely described dishes, it is suggested that you consult one of the many cook books of other lands which may be found in most libraries or book stores.

The subject, eating customs, was purposely chosen because we all must eat, and most will agree that eating is a social process by which acquaintances may become friends. Simply written, it is hoped that this collection will assist those who wish to be at ease with foreign hosts. At least, it should lead to a more pleasant and relaxed interaction between peoples of different cultures.

Manners are an important part of enjoyment. One cannot feel at ease without some understanding of the culture in which he or she finds himself or herself. Yet, over-studied or stilted manners may tend to break down natural friendly relations. It is better to be more natural and to rely upon one's own good manners than to copy others without fully understanding them.

Some foods will be more difficult to accept at times than the manner in which they are eaten. For instance, to some these foods may seem strange and unpalatable, they may even revolt some senses, while to others they may be delicacies: rats, cats, dogs, horses, eels, grasshoppers, worms, snakes, raw blood, lamb's eyes, raw meat, bird's nests, rotting cheeses and others. Many people cannot imagine, on the other hand, eating cottage cheese, corn on the cob, oysters, puddings, or drinking weak coffee, cocktails or ice water. Nourishment is not always the major concern and may give way to custom or tradition. Delicacies may simply mean that certain foods, or a special food, are scarce in a given area.

The enjoyment and contentment of eating is measured by what one has been taught to accept as good or bad. Religion has a profound effect on what we eat and at times one finds it difficult to separate religious and socially cultural reasons for our behavioral patterns of eating. In almost all societies the act of eating is an important part of the culture, of the family unit, of friendships and often of political and business communications.

In this research, a pattern of sameness emerges although customs may differ. The origin of customs may stem from the same root reason. Customs may shed light on how a certain peoples react to each other and to outsiders, and how they are changing as their family customs change, and how they reflect the changing world about them.

Almost all of the information is derived from interviews with visitors to the United States, although some notes have been added from personal travels. The author thanks all of those who contributed so willingly, not only for the written material, but also for the pleasant hours spent both here and abroad with interesting persons who contributed to this study.

Obviously, not all countries could be included, even if just for physical space. Therefore, countries were chosen to give an idea of some of the customs of those areas around the world. Also, the reader will appreciate the fact that not all of the customs of any one country could be included, as cultural patterns differ within the countries themselves, both because of geography and class status.

May your eating habits be tasty, interesting, healthy, and forever add to your knowledge, understanding and happiness. And may this book help you to recognize the cultural cues so that you may follow your hosts and feel comfortable with them.

ACKNOWLEDGEMENTS

The author wishes to thank the following friends from other countries for their help in contributing information about customs in their homeland.

It is only by understanding how people live in other countries and their values that we can begin to develop a more harmonious world for all of us. For this reason, this book is dedicated to them and to other venturesome people who cross boundaries, both geographical and mental, to communicate about their culture and to learn from others.

Radia Abdulla
Moshe Abramovici
Yosif Aleissa

Sergio Arguedos
Nabil Ao-Zamel
Dieter Baier

Rita Bainridge
Margarita Bazo
Nicolas Butler

Greg Camacho
Mansour Chamily
Into Chamnongphanij

Judy Chang
Su-Wen Chang
Chang Kuk Cho

Chung Farrell
Han-Ping Chung
Viviana Coello

Jorge David
Joseph El Chamily
Pina Ely

Nagibottoman Essed
Khalil Farah
Rocio Lascurain Farrell

Elena Felicio
Afereti Fetiu
Nancy Fruttero

Bettina Gerischer
Arpad Giorfi
Isaac Gzamenah

Nadia Hussein Hassona
Tunde Hidvegi
Marilyn Hoalim

Michelle Houbin
Aziz Hussain
Mohammed Jahadi

Marina Jilka
Karen Jones
Bengt Jonsson

Myrtha Joseph
Alvar Kauti
Tammy Ko

Mooi Lam
Amin Leiman
Li-Li Liu

Louise Lyon
Gilberto Malakauskas
Sonia Miranda

Zahara Mohamed
Norazian Mohd-Thani
Josian Mokelv

Ayo Muri
David Muumbi
Fahim Nasraty

Eieng Lim Ngee
Arie Norlander
Marilena Perrone

Ahm Qutubuddin
Rangasami
Swarne Ratnasoma

Ayse Sazak
Hamid Shahid
Masasumi Shimbo

Oscar Simon
Herbert Vargas
Patricia Villanueva

Ruth Thamayanthi Williams
Mable Wu
Maria Eugenia Zuberan

AFGHANISTAN

Afghanistan, whose capital is Kabul, has as its principal languages Persian (or Dari) and Pustu. Some Turki is spoken in the Northern region. The people are racially mixed and the population is about seventeen million. From the map, one can realize Afghanistan's relationship to other countries and understand it strategic position throughout history. The country has an unpeaceful history which includes numerous invasions. Past rules have included Arab, Persian, Turkish, British and a period under Ghengis Kahn. The climate is that of cold winters and hot, dry summers. The official religion is Islamic.

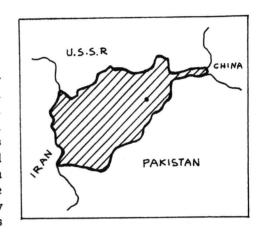

Women have worn the traditional Moslim veil. In fact, for centuries there has been turmoil over the veil, or chadri, which was made of finely pleated cotton or silk and which covered the wearer from head to ankle length. Attached to it was a hood which covered the face almost entirely. It is almost impossible to see through a chadri.

Women have stayed home while men have shopped, even when the shopping was to buy lengths of cloth for their dresses. As early as 1929 King Amanullah attempted to liberate women from their dress and substation of their culture, but then, and later, attempts failed. At time, revolutions even erupted because of the strong feelings against such liberalizing of women, and women seldom fought to bring about any charges.

Customs in Afghanistan die hard and you should always take traditions seriously, never discussing that they be changed unless you are prepared for fierce opposition.

Afghans are a friendly people and their customs will be interesting to a visitor. They will gladly discuss their way of life and welcome your curiosity.

In the privacy of a home Afghan woman will proudly show visiting women their children, their clothes, and even their jewelry with no thought of timidly hiding their features or emotions.

At present many Afghans are westernized and in some homes customs are a blend of old and new. Changes are developing daily, but many customs remain somewhat the same. To be a guest in a home may be an interesting and pleasant experience.

Dinner is usually eaten about 8:30 or 9 p.m. The guest should arrive early. In fact, guests may arrive anytime after two in the afternoon, the idea being to visit, not just to eat. If you do not know when to arrive, it is polite to ask your host when you will be expected. Dinner guests do not bring gifts or flowers.

The person who greets you at the door may be the one who has invited you, or the father, or sons. Women usually do not do this. You will then be escorted to a salon or living room which may be in Western style. If it is a traditional home you may eat in the same room where you visit. This room is called "Doshak".

If the women speak English (or your language) they will join you for conversation, which may include all subjects except sex, which is controlled by religion and should not be mentioned. Because the use of alcoholic drinks is prohibited by religion none will be served. You may be served fruits, on a large dish from which you will serve yourself on a smaller plate and eat with a fork and knife. This is accompanied by some fruit juice, tea or coffee. (Fruit is sometimes eaten with fingers but usually not when there are guests present). A bowl of water will be brought to wash your hands if you have eaten with your fingers. The ladies will lead all to the dining room.

Seating may vary, the host and hostess may sit together or by the side of the guests. The hostess's place is usually nearest to the kitchen.Children usually eat separately. Everything will be on the table, cutlery in the Western style, plates and the food. There may be a table cloth, usually decorated, or place mats and napkins or sometimes paper napkins.

A prayer, which can be of any religion, or something made up for the occasion, is often lead by the guest.

A platter is placed near the guest who is asked to begin. Help yourself, but not too generously, as you will be encouraged to eat more later. Guests should eat to show that they enjoy the food.

Conversation may encompass various subjects but is usually sparse while eating. The food may be complimented and recipes may be requested.

Some typical meals will consist of "palau" (brown rice) or "chalau" (white rice). Chalau being the most commonly served; Persian bread, no butter; various types of salad, fresh vegetables and chutneys. Desert is often "fermi," a white pudding, or jello. Water and soft drinks, usually no coffee, are served.

At the end of the meal all say thanks to God for everything. Then, either the group remains at the table to sit, talk and have tea, other sweets or fruits, or re-enter the living room to have tea, candies, salted bits, nuts or other snacks.

When leaving, you will repeatedly be asked to stay, even to spend the night. Your excuse may be that all need to get up to go to work in the morning. But you must stay at least one half hour up to two hours depending upon the evening. Never leave before one half hour minimum. It is polite to thank your hosts and say that the food was good. In the native language thank you is, "Tashakor". Do not send a note, but you may send flowers. Before leaving the country it will be appreciated if you call in person to say goodbye. You may write from home and invite them to visit.

In the more traditional home, all will sit in the same room, on pillows, and the food will be placed on dishes on the floor to be eaten with fingers from the main dish. A prayer is also said. Hands are washed before and after eating.

Palau

Put rice (it is white rice cooked with broth until it turns brown) on first. Add raisins, carrots, chicken or beef. Numerous kinds of sauces (adding more spices) are served in different dishes. Each family may make this dish differently with more fruits, etc.

Chalau

It is pure rice, no carrots, raisins or meat, to be used with different sauce dishes.

ARGENTINA

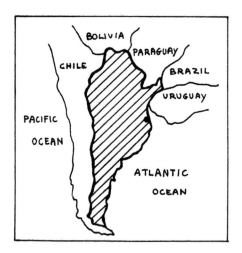

Buenos Aires, a very European type city, is the capital of this second largest country in South America. Argentina's climate varies depending upon the area as there are mountains, lowlands, windy steppes and rain sections. The Pampa is the most fertile part of the country, having some of the richest top soil in the world. Argentine beef is famous and the Gauchos are sometimes likened to the early Western United States cowboys, Gaucho life being more colorful and more permanent.

Argentina's population is about one half "middle class", and is a mixture of Italian and Spanish predominately, with some English, other Europeans, Arabs and people of Jewish decent. Pure blooded Indians are a minority. Most of the people are Catholic. Spanish is the official language but Italian, English, French and German are spoken by many. Rule was Spanish until independence in 1816.

The dinner hour may be from 8 p.m. to 10 p.m., or even until 11 p.m. in the night, depending upon the family and the custom of living or hours of work. Restaurants are often open all night for full meals.

A guest is expected to arrive about ten minutes early or on time. Sometimes a servant or the mother or father of the family may open the door and welcome the guest, then escort him to the salon. In the more traditional or rural areas the guests may go directly to the large kitchen family room where all is very informal and very friendly. In the salon, or living room, one may be offered a glass of vermouth, plain, or with soda and icé, or soda water, but seldom whiskey. Hors d'oeuvres are served and consist of salami, cheese and olives. Here all chat together about one half hour. In the more traditional homes there will probably be no drinks served. When it is time to go to the dining room, the host will generally lead the way.

The dining table will have a cloth table cloth with napkins, and the usual silverware. The host will sit at the head of the table, the hostess at the opposite end, guests along the sides.

Soup is sometimes served, especially in colder weather. The soup may contain corn with meat and other vegetables. Salad is eaten with the meal, dressing is mostly vinegar and oil and is mixed at the table by each person. Dinner will always have meat, the most popular being steak, which is often considered the best in the world.

A thick dinner steak may be so tender that you can almost cut it with a knife. The meal includes vegetables of various types, potatoes cooked in many ways. Argentines sometimes eat corn on the cob as is done in the United States. Dessert is usually fresh fruit.

Because meat is so popular in Argentina, steak is often cooked in many ways. Originally, meat was served with almost every meal and until recently was one of the least expensive foods in the country. One of many recipes follows.

Churrasco Rebosado

To the yolks of four eggs add about one and one half cups of flour and beat until it is not lumpy. Add one half cup of milk and some crushed garlic, a little salt and pepper, some marjorum. Then beat the whites of the eggs and add them to the mixture. Take six medium size steaks or fillets of beef and cover them with the mixture. Get about one cup of olive oil very, very hot and fry the meat in it. Do not cook for more than two or three minutes on each side.

The Gauchos used to barbecue the meat over hot coals or cook it over an open fire. Probably many different ways of eating meat have never been recorded as the Gaucho was not one to cook by a book.

Grace, or a prayer, may be said, but some families begin the meal without it. When you finish a dish, the fork and knife are placed in a crossed position on the plate, prongs down. The spoon may be left in any position. A guest may offer to help clear the table if it seems appropriate.

Conversation at dinner is pleasant, can cover all subjects, and often does. Usually the dinner ends happily and all return to the salon where coffee and liqueur (especially in winter) are served. A guest should remain for at least one half hour and up to about one and one half hours depending upon the circumstances.

When leaving, a "Gracias", or thank you, is all that is expected: no gift, no flowers, no thank you note, and it is not customary to invite your hosts to your hotel for a meal to reciprocate. To telephone and say goodbye and again mention the pleasant evening to them is considered polite. A letter from home to report about your travels and to invite your hosts to visit, if you wish, will be appreciated.

Empanada

This is a traditional food which is made with ground beef, green onions, eggs, green olives, raisins, salt, red pepper, cumin and a little vegetable oil. Prepare and mix together. Flatten quite thin, a piece of plain dough on a slab or board and fill it with about three tablespoons of the mixture, then fold over the dough and press together carefully the edges. Finally, fry all of this in very hot oil. Eat while very hot.

Dough can be made of flour, tepid water, salt, butter and a little yeast.

Mate'

Argentine mate' is drunk as tea is in most countries, usually in the afternoon. The beverage at mealtimes is wine or water and goes well with the cooking which is mostly in the Italian style. Mate' is drunk with a straw from a special small cup-like container.

Locro

This is a type of popular soup. Into water put beef, pork, sausage, all cut into one inch or a little larger squares; also vegetables, dry beans which can be various types mixed, herbs, parsley, pepper and salt, celery, onion and one tomato. Boil very slowly for about two hours and one half. Do not strain.

Great rivers
of Argentina

AUSTRALIA

Australia is the smallest continent in the world, but in reality it is a very large nation. Its capital is Canberra. There is much flat, barren, arid land in Australia and great ranches over vast areas where sheep and cattle are raised. The climate varies greatly from desert to tropical, with an annual rainfall up to 100 inches in some parts of the country. The population is mostly of British origin with other immigrants, mainly from Europe, arriving more recently. There are also Australian aborigines who live mainly in the north. In the 18th Century many convicts from Britain were early settlers. These were often convicted for what today would scarcely be considered a crime, and these were later emancipated as more immigrants arrived. Today, Australia is a member of the British Commonwealth.

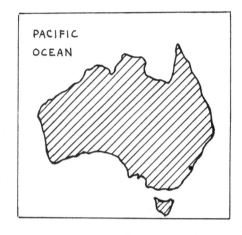

The dinner hour is usually about 6 o'clock and eating customs are approximately the same all through the nation. You may arrive about one half hour early if asked for a "six o'clock dinner", or you may be on time, but never late. Guests do not bring gifts or flowers, but you may bring wine or beer. However, it is not customary to do so and, in fact, some families would prefer you do not as they just wish you to accept their hospitality. Beer will be served in the living room during the pre-dinner hour which will often last about one half hour. In the dining room the table will have a cloth and linen napkins, and seating will usually be informal. Grace is said in some homes, but not in most. The atmosphere is simple and friendly and one is encouraged to feel at ease. Manners are generally similar to those of England or America. The food may be placed before you already on your individual plate, in which case you may mention that you do not wish too much, especially if there are foods you do not like. This will not be considered impolite if you eat all that is offered after you have designated the amount. Guests may offer to help serve if they wish. The fork is held in the left hand and the knife in the right, while both are used together. Dinner may include a salad, eaten with the rest of the meal, such as lettuce and tomato with a mayonnaise dressing. Then there will be meat; steak, lamb, fish or chicken. Meat is eaten at each meal during the day. Vegetables of many kinds and potatoes, which are very popular, and dessert will round out the meal. Australians fit the description of "meat and potato" people. Desserts may be fruits, custards, ice cream, tapioca or cake, and beverages are tea, beer, coffee or wine. There are a few spices used in the preparation of the dishes and thus the food is mild. Conversation is easy and plentiful and may be about any subject.

When you have finished eating a course, your knife and fork should be placed on your plate side by side. When soup is served, this should be spooned away from your body and sipped quietly from the side of the spoon, never from the front or point. At informal, and especially out-of-door meals, you may be handed a plate and asked to "help yourself" from a central table. You should then carry your plate with the food to a table where guests will be seated for eating and join them, usually simply choosing the most convenient empty chair.

After returning to the living room tea will be served and this may be accompanied by cookies. You may leave about 10:30 or 11 p.m.

A thank you when leaving is all that is expected, no note, no gift, no flowers. You should call, however, when leaving the country to say goodbye and then write when you are home to tell about your voyage and thank them, if you wish, or invite them to visit your country.

Toad-in-the-Hole (Originally from England but very popular throughout Australia.)

1 1/2 cups of flour sifted carefully
1 tablespoon salt
1 beaten egg
1/2 teaspoon baking powder
2 cups of milk
About 3 cups of sliced cooked chicken or 5-6 slices cooked roast
 beef
About 1/4 cup chopped parsley
Small amount of pepper

Mix flour and salt and baking powder in a bowl and add the milk, egg and beat together. Put the chicken or roast beef into a buttered casserole and cover with parsley, pepper and the other half of the salt if you have not mixed all the salt already. Then pour the flour mixture over the top and put into the oven. Bake for one hour at about 350 degree oven. Serve in the casserole.

BANGLADESH

Dacca is the captial of Bangladesh which is one of the most densely populated countries in the world. Bengali is spoken by most of the inhabitants and most are Muslims, though some are Hindus, Buddhists, Christians and Animists. English is spoken in most of the areas. The country is multi-racial including Aryans, Arabs, Dravidians, Mongolians, Persians, and Turks. Bangladesh is a comparatively new nation but it has an old hsitory. It was ruled by Mongol (Muslim), British, and was formed when West Pakistan split off from East Pakistan. The story of Bangladesh is full of turmoil, political strife and a desire to be independent. The climate is tropical, with monsoons and some of the highest rainfalls in the world. Its rivers are abundant and floods are common, sometimes hindering travel.

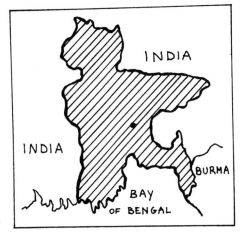

In the traditional custom, when someone is invited to dinner, a host family member will go to the guest's house to invite him or her, as there are few or no phones in the villages. He may say: "Come around eight o'clock." The guest can arrive up to one half hour early or one half hour late. One may bring a gift, such as food, in the form of sweets, or a dessert, especially if it is homemade.

When a guest arrives, the greeting is "Assalamu Alaikum". The father, or head of the family, will greet the guest at the door and escort him or her either to the salon or living room, or to a general room. Traditionally, if there are men only, the wife will not enter the living room. About one half hour is devoted to talking. Because of the Muslim religion, no liquor will be served. The wife will go with the females, usually in the kitchen room, or a bedroom. If the visitor is foreign, both males and females may join in the living room. On occasion, if the guest is Christian, he may be served some alcoholic beverage. More frequently, the host will offer a glass of water. Traditionally all might eat in the same room, since there would be no separate dining area.

There is usually a servant, although the hostess may have worked to prepare the dinner for most of the day. The servant may often stay in the kitchen. When the meal is of the older traditional custom, the food will be served on a cloth on the floor and the platters or bowls placed in the center of the group. Women would eat later and by themselves. The host would suggest that all wash their hands and someone will pour the water for each person; there is soap and a towel. Then the eating begins and in both traditional or modern

- 16 -

homes, one says: "Bismilah hur Rahman nur Rahim", which means, "Starting with the name of God who is most graceful."

All fingers are used for eating, but the right hand only. There are no napkins. Rice is eaten first and is usually served by the host on each plate with a spoon. There will be vegetables fried in oil called "Bhajhi". Vegetables are spiced. Take some vegetables with your fingers, mix with rice and eat. Take some rice and eat. Take small servings as rice will be used for other foods also. A main dish may be curry with fried fish and vegetables; this may be eaten first. Water is served as the beverage.

The guest begins to eat, the most important guest first and this can become an occasion for great deference, each one saying, "After you!". The host may serve chicken curry to each plate and you must use your rice to pick up the juices. Finger eating can be very graceful when one has learned how to do it well.

Conversation at meals is sparse as it is assumed that this was finished before dinner. Talk is usually just to ask for more water, rice, etc. Eating should be a quiet process and it is considered very impolite to make any noise.

After the curry dish, there will be soup called "Dahl". There is usually a side dish of salad but one does not necessarily need to eat this.

You will find that the host will be very insistent that you eat more. It is polite to say no and to insist back, even to raising your arms in protest. However, the host family will like it if you eat heartily.

Sometimes after dinner hot milk may be served, especially if the host family has a cow. Desserts are homemade but are not generally baked (as many villagers do not own an oven). The sweets may be yogurt or fruit.

In the modern setting there will be straight back chairs and sofas in the living room. There are separate rooms for talk and for dining and there will be a dining table and chairs. Here, you will wash your hands in a small room using a basin and running water.

The lady of the house serves everything in the more modern home, but she will eat later even if the guests include women who, if foreign, may eat with the men. In both traditional and modern homes, with fingers or with cutlery, it is very important to wash your hands before and after each meal.

After dinner conversation in the living room may resume for about one hour. It is usually polite to leave about 10 or 11 p.m. When leaving, thank you is "Dhon-no-bahd", and goodbye is "Khuda Hafiz", which means, "God be with you." No other thanks is needed, no note, no gift, no flowers.

You may invite the family to your hotel, but they will undoubtedly decline. When you leave the country, call or visit to say goodbye and invite them to visit your country and you. It is always appreciated if you send a card or note now and then after returning.

Kabab is a very popular dish.

Kabab (Kabob)

2 pounds of ground beef	1/4 teaspoon curry powder
1/2 medium sized chopped onion	1/4 teaspoon cayenne
2 cloves garlic, chopped	1/4 teaspoon ginger
1 green chili, chopped	1/4 teaspoon black pepper
1/4 spoon salt	1/4 pound sweet peas, cooked and
1/4 cup bread crumbs	mashed

Mix all the ingredients thoroughly in a bowl and make flat round molded pieces, size as desired. Broil one side for about 20 minutes, then the other side for about 15 minutes, or until browned. Makes about 24 pieces or enough for 6 people.

Corma (this may be made with chicken, beef or lamb)

(chicken with yogurt)

1 medium size chicken (or equivalent in other meat)	1/4 teaspoon cinnamon powder
1/2 cup yogurt	1/4 teaspoon black pepper
1/4 teaspoon salt	3 or 4 cloves
1 medium size onion chopped	2 or 3 bay leaves
1/4 teaspoon ginger powder	2 or 3 cardimon or 1/4 teaspoon powder
1/4 teaspoon garlic powder	1/4 cube butter

Cut chicken into 8 pieces, place in a bowl, mix all the ingredients together except the butter with the chicken, coating it well. Leave it for one half hour to marinate, in the refrigerator or in a cool place. Melt butter in a frying pan, with medium heat, put the chicken pieces into it, not using any of the extra juice; stir until a little brownish, then add the left over juice to the pan. Stir for one minute, cover and cook for ten minutes, repeat this process four times or until the chicken is cooked. Serves four people.

These two dishes, served with steamed rice, make a delicious meal.

BOLIVIA

Bolivia is one of the few land-locked countries in South America. Its topography is dramatic, including a section of the Andes and the Amazon-Chaco lowlands. Customs are maintained from historical times and the people are racially mixed, with mostly Spanish and Indian. The civilization under the early Indians was highly advanced.

La Paz, the capital, is the highest city in the world and, in fact, visitors often find it difficult to breathe at such an altitude. Although access to the ocean has been lost, as a result of part of its turbulent military history, the country still has a rare beauty and a pleasant population. The Republic is named after Simon Bolivar, the famous hero liberator of Latin America. Most Bolivians are Catholic, but Indians still retain some traditional religious practices which they combine with Christianity. In some areas tap water may not be good for a visitor to drink, although one need not be concerned in the large cities.

Pure bred Indians number approximately 60% of the population. The Indians have very colorful hues in their skin, a creamy tan with deep red cheeks showing through and sometimes the children seem to radiate a navy glow. Clothing worn by the native women is unique and also very colorful. Partly because of the altitude and climate, there are many layers of clothing. There are bright outer skirts which are full and dip slightly in the front at the hem covering many underskirts to add to fullness. Over this is a shawl of still more colors, usually covering a white blouse and on this, over the shawl, is a colorful carry all which often contains an infant. Market places are a special joy for the photographer as customs and produce blend in an array of rainbow hues. But the most fascinating part of the native dress is the hat which is worn by every Cholita, or Bolivian Indian woman, and is a derbie. Men dress more conservatively and are distinguished by their Lluchu, a knitted colorful cap with ear flaps, or by their Fedoras.

The Indians are somewhat shy to strangers at first, but they are friendly and their social interaction, even though directed by tradition, is festive and they are often known to have quite a rollicking time at week's end, or at holiday times. They maintain most of their original customs and their food contains a good proportion of corn or maize. Living is hard and age shows early in their lined but attractive faces. To dine in a private home will be a

pleasant experience and customs are similar to those found in other
South American and European countries.

Guests should arrive on time or not more than ten minutes late. Gifts
are not usually brought, but they are acceptable, especially flowers
or wine, but not any type of food.

The hostess will greet the guest at the door, then she will generally
leave the guest with the host in the salon or living room. If there
is a servant, the hostess will remain in the living room also. This
is the time for talk and refreshments of wine and beer. In the
villages, the traditional drink is "Chicha", made from corn; less
strong than wine, but not always easily digested by one not accustomed
to it. You should only take one or two glasses, usually one glass
while still in the living room and the other at the table. Your glass
will always be refilled, so it is best to drink slowly.

In the older tradition, roasted corn or peas are served; this is
called "Haba". In the cities there are seldom any tidbits such as
potato chips, or nuts served unless for a special party. After 15 or
20 minutes the hostess will announce dinner and lead all to the dining
room. The host will sit at one end of the table, the hostess at the
other, guests at the right; women usually sit together or all may "sit
where you wish".

Salad (entrada) is usually served at lunch, but not at dinner. Lunch
will consist of salad, soup, a main dish of meat and vegetables, and
the second dish (segundo) or dessert. Dinner may have a main dish of
meat, rice, vegetables and sometimes dessert. The cutlery or
silverware is the same as in Europe or America and eating customs are
similar.

In La Paz, and especially in some cold cities, coffee is always served
at the end of a meal. During the meal a soft drink or wine is used.

To toast, one uses the traditional South American "Salud" but in Bolivia
it is usually followed by a sentence explaining why one is saying it:
"To my old friend", etc.

Children from about the age of eight may eat with the family and
friends. Table conversation is friendly and often wide ranged. At
the end of the meal one says, "Gracias" (thank you). The host will
probably reply, "Provech", which means, "I hope the meal will be
useful for you." All this is done while still at the dining table.

Because the time at the table may be quite long, if you should wish to
leave for a moment, say "Permiso" (excuse me), and return quietly.
Either the group will remain at the table for a lengthy talk, or will
move back to the living room where you should remain for at least one
half hour, but not much longer.

When leaving, a verbal thanks is adequate. One does not write a note as a rule, but you may do so if you wish. A letter after you have returned to your country is the accepted form of thanks. This letter should tell about your trip and be filled with news about yourself. It may contain an invitation for them to visit your homeland.

Empanada is a popular food and varies in the way it is made from country to country, and sometimes within the countries. See the recipe under Argentina. Even though meat is important, the Empanada, which is eaten in many South American countries, is often made with no meat here. Cheese is substituted for the meat filling. These empanadas have a delicate flavor and are served piping hot. You may buy them at the train stops on the road from Lake Titicaca to La Paz and you will remember the taste and this trip with nostalgia.

BRAZIL

Brasilia, a modern city in the central part of the country is Brazil's capital.Portuguese is the official language, because of the historical Portuguese influence. Foreign rule was Portuguese, but the country is now a federative republic. Africans and local Indians blend to create the population mix. In more recent years, many Italians, Germans, and Japanese have made Brazil their home.

English is the second language, but a visitor would be wise to learn some Portuguese to communicate easily. Also, Spanish is understood by most. As in many South American nations, there is a marked difference between rich and poor.

The country is warm and humid due to heavy rainfalls and the Amazon River; which is also a reason for so much damp, flat land area. Most of Brazil is in the tropics. Densely forested lowlands cover much of the country's interior, where succulent jungle fruits flourish; a semi-arid scrubland area is in the northeast where native foods are more sparse. In the west and south, there are mountains and hills where cattle and sheep graze in the area of Rio Grande do Sul and, finally, there is the long coastal zone where seafood is abundant.

Although there is much modern development and new road systems help unite the different regions, many of the distinctive traditions, music, and local color of the various parts of Brazil remain for the visitor to note and enjoy.

The geographical areas of Brazil differ greatly in climate and character and, because of this, life styles from region to region. Along the Amazon River there are Indian tribes who live entirely off the land and whose customs have changed very little through the ages. In this jungle climate life is simple and food is either grown or hunted. Contrasting this is the life in large cities such as Rio de Janeiro or Sao Paulo where the pace is accelerated and customs are similar to those of Europe. Brasilia has a style of its own, a city which was man-made at a precise time for a precise reason, constructed to be the capital of the country and situated inland to promote growth in that direction. It was literally carved out of the jungle and architecturally planned as a modern and unique group of buildings to house governmental offices. Originally there was little housing and though many units have been added in recent years, many people still regard this as a city to which people commute to work but live and entertain elsewhere. Of the cities, Brasilia is the political hub,

Rio is the fun-loving, Sao Paulo is the city of economic progress and Bahia is known for its traditional charm and warm friendliness.

When guests are invited they should arrive on time, or a few minutes early. A gift to the host family is not necessary, but if one can bring a basket of strawberries it will be very much appreciated; candy or champagne is also welcome. It is not customary to bring flowers. Usually a female servant will greet you at the door. Cocktails are served in the salon or living room and the drinks will be accompanied by a variety of crackers, cheeses, fruits, sweets, nuts, possibly strawberries on cream and other tidbits. A cart is often wheeled in and you may help yourself from it.

When going to the dining room any member of the family may lead the way. You may sit where you wish. The host and hostess usually sit together at one side of the table. There is a table cloth, napkins, the usual silverware and plates.

The meal begins with a salad, followed by soup, meats, fish, chicken, rice, potatoes and other vegetables. Beverages may consist of water, milk, orange juice, coca cola, wine, or guaraná, a drink made from local fruits. A servant usually prepares the meal, which often is served at the table by passing it around. After dinner, coffee is served in the living room, or another beverage if the guest wishes. A guest should stay at least one half hour after the meal and use judgment about leaving, as this time is very flexible.

You may thank the family and invite them to your home, hotel, or a restaurant for dinner as you partake your leave. No other thanks is needed; no gift, no note, no flowers, although it would not be impolite to send some fruits or candy, but not flowers. A letter from your homeland after you have returned is most welcome.

Feijoado (pronounced feshuada)

1 pound dry beef (whole) - Boil 10 minutes and drain
1 pound smoked ham hocks (whole)
1 pound hot Italian sausage
1 pound smoked Polish sausage - sliced 1/2" thick
1 pound pig's feet (fresh, whole)
1 large onion quartered
2 bay leaves
4 large cloves garlic
1 pound black beans
Olive oil

Wash the beans and place in a large, heavy pot. Combine all the ingredients except garlic, cover with one inch water. Cook over high flame until boils, simmer for two hours or until beans are cooked (firm). Remove dry beef, dice more or less and discard fat, return to pot. Remove hocks, discard bones and skin, return meat to pot.

Remove pig's feet, discard bones and return meat to pot. Discard onions and bay leaves. Skim off any surface fat. Crush garlic, saute' in small amount of olive oil until golden, add beans and mix. Don't add salt, as it is already tasty enough from the two kinds of sausages. Serve with rice. Goes well with finely cut collard greens sautéed in garlic and olive oil.

CANADA

Ottawa is the capital of Canada, the second largest country in the world in terms of land area. Its climate varies as it extends to the North Pole and from the Atlantic to the Pacific. It is cool with long cold winters which is why most of its population lives within 100 miles of its southern border. Most Canadians are of British or French origin and their major religions are Protestant and Catholic. The natives in the far north, like those in Alaska, have a traditional set of cultural patterns, but the majority of Canadian's customs relate very closely to those of the French (in

the French speaking section), British and American. Rule was British and French with the French defeated but leaving considerable influence. Immigrants have come and continue to enter from all areas of the world. There is little difference between Canadian and U.S. spoken English. Their French is said to be pure as it has remained much the same as it was when brought to the New World. Dining customs resemble English, America or French.

Dinner may be eaten at five, six, seven or sometimes later. One is expected to arrive on time. A small gift may be brought to the host family if desired. When you arrive at the door, it may be opened by any member of the family who will welcome you and show you to the salon or living room. Here, cocktails are served, sometimes accompanied by hors d'oeuvres, or you may be offered tea or coffee. As a rule, this will last about one half hour.

As you enter the dining room you will find the table with a cloth, silverware and setting the same as in Western Europe or the United States. The father and mother sit at opposite ends of the table, guests to the sides. Sometimes, instead of cloths, placemats and paper napkins are used.

Naturally, the food in the French section will more closely resemble that of the cooking in France. Restaurants are well known and serve varied and delicious dishes.

Sometimes families say Grace, sometimes they do not. This depends on the individual family.

Wine is served often, but many times when children eat with adults, water may be served in its place. The father usually begins eating as the mother is often serving (unless there is a servant). A guest may offer to help serve, clear the plates, etc., and may or may not be allowed to do so.

Generally, a Canadian meal consists of soup or salad or just salad with the main dish. Beef is popular and served with potatoes and vegetables, bread and butter. Dessert may be apple pie, ice cream, cake, or the most usual fruits such as peaches, plums, pears and apples, often eaten with cheese.

Table conversation is friendly and can be about any subject in both French and non-French areas.

Coffee and alcoholic beverages are served after dinner in the living room. Here one should stay at least half an hour and up to two or three hours, this being flexible and left to good judgment.

Thank you notes are seldom sent in Canada, a thank you at the door when leaving is sufficient. You may send a card when leaving the country or a letter from your home when you return inviting them to visit and telling them about your travels.

Since recipes would resemble those from France, England or America, none are included here.

CHINA (PEOPLE'S REPUBLIC)

The third largest country in the world
is the People's Republic of China.
Peking is its capital and two thirds of
the country is in mountain or desert
areas with only about one tenth of the
land available for cultivation. Almost
all the population lives in the fertile
plains or deltas in the east. Summers
are hot and humid and winters are dry
and can be very cold, although the
weather varies in different sections of
the country. There are monsoons and
some flooding occurs. China is the most
populous country in the world and
includes several non-Chinese groups
such as the Uighurs, Muslims, Mongols, Manchus, Chuangs, and Tibetans.
Most religions are tolerated but are not as prominent as they were
before communism. Originally the strongest of these were
Confucianists, Buddhists, Taoists and Muslims. The official language
is the Peking dialect of Mandarin Chinese.

China's history is very old, very colorful and very civilized. Under
some dynasties culture advanced to great heights; literature, art,
craftsmanship and philosophy were some of the most important fields of
development. More recently a need for scientific development has been
recognized and is an important consideration of the present
government.

The people have suffered hardships due to their great numbers, lack of
adequate food during lean years, and political revolutionary changes.
There is constant change in China and new directions of thought, but
many customs remain from the traditional China of old.

If a visitor has a native friend, or makes a friend while visiting
China, he or she may very likely be invited to dinner in a private
home. The Chinese enjoy meeting Americans and many speak English
which they may have learned by themselves or from someone who had
studied abroad. Unknown to many is the fact that the "Voice of
America" program was heard through the years of governmental changes
which gave to them an opportunity to know the outside world. The
natives are happy to welcome visitors and appreciate any opportunity
to practice their English.

Chinese cuisine is world renown. In China of old, chefs often led
important but precarious lives. They could be killed if a dish was
not good or if it became too repetitious. When they were good they
were highly respected. Meals sometimes lasted for three days and
special foods were imported from areas which were recognized for

producing the best flavor.   The scarcity of food encouraged the development of many recipes with unique ingredients. Dogs, cats and rats have all been used in cooking. Bird's nests, for example, were picked near the sea as sea moss is used to build the nests. The most desired nests are those which have not yet been soiled, the others are carefully washed and cleaned before using. Bird nest soup, in the time of Genghis Khan, was used because there was not enough food, and the swallows' nests contained food which the parent birds stored for their young, thus they were nourishing.

Meals are friendly and the atmosphere is jovial. Wine is served and each guest may be seated by the host drinking to him. Toasts are often made and the usual word used is "Gampei".

When the host decides it is time to begin eating, he lifts his chopsticks, says "ch'ing" and all begin to eat. Ivory chopsticks are the most frequently used, with one small porcelain spoon for soup. Wine is sipped throughout the meal. The host may move from one table to another in a large gathering.

Meals may have numerous courses and it is wise not to over indulge at the beginning of a dinner. Noodles (or spaghetti) are basic, and a point of interest which may not be known to all is that noodles or spaghetti were brought (it is believed by Marco Polo) to Italy from China; rice was brought to China from Italy. Cooking varies greatly from north to south. The more northern area is often considered to have the best food.

Often a meal will begin with spare ribs, egg rolls and other tidbits. The better dishes often follow the lesser ones. Beer, wine or tea may be served, and tea almost always at end of the meal. Delicacies may consist of fried dry lillies and other items which are unusual to many western country recipes.

Low round tables are usually used with many bowls of various sizes, all filled with different foods or sauces. Soya sauce is used with most foods.

HOW TO HOLD THE STICKS

CERAMIC SPOON

BOWLS

IVORY STICKS

Many Chinese dishes, when served in other countries, as with many imported foods, are altered to fit the local taste, or adjusted to the ingredients available. Therefore, the same dish many have one taste in its native land and another elsewhere. A true Chinese meal, in its native setting, can be a rare and delightful experience.

You may send a note of thanks or a letter from home but flowers are not expected and white flowers never should be brought or sent as they are associated with death. White is the color for funerals. Brides never wear white--their color is red, which depicts happiness.

Sweet and Sour Fish (Shanghai)

A 3 cups peanut oil
B 1 to 1 1/2 pound porgy or bass
C 1/2 cup shrimp diced
D 1/2 cup peas
E 1 tablespoon light soy sauce
F 1 tablespoon cherry
G 3 tablespoons catsup
H 1 tablespoon sugar

I 1/2 teaspoon vinegar
J 2 tablespoons corn starch
K 1 tomato
L 1 teasp. corn starch mixed
  with 2 tablespoons water
M 1 teaspoon salt
N dash pepper

Preparation:
1. Mix L, M, N thoroughly
2. Slash both sides of B diagonally at 2 inch intervals, rub with L-N mixture. Roll in J so that B is coated with a thin layer.
3. Mix E, F, G, H, I and 1 teaspoon J.
4. Mix C with additional 1/2 teaspoon cornstarch and dash of salt.
5. Place K in boiling water for a few seconds, remove, peel and cut into cubs.

Cooking:
1. Heat A to 325°; deep fry B until golden brown (about 5 minutes). Remove to dish.
2. Heat additional 1 tablespoon oil, stir-fry C 1 to 2 minutes, add D.
3. Add E, K, J mixture, stir until thickened.
4. Pour over B and serve. Garnish with K.

More eating customs will be found in the sections of Taiwan (Republic of China) and Hong Kong.

COSTA RICA

Costa Rica's capital is San Jose, which
rules over the second smallest Central
American Republic. It is a mountainous
country with hot tropical weather in the
lowlands and medium temperatures in the
high lands. Most of the people live in
these highlands. Of almost total Europe
descent, mainly Spanish, the people are
generally Catholic. Indians and black
descendants of Jamaican laborers makeup
the remaining population. Spanish is
the official language, but a Jamaican
dialect of English is spoken
extensively. Rule was Spanish with an
independent, agrarian social life.
Differences between rich and poor have
not been so marked as in some other Latin American countries.

People who live in the city of San Jose are avid card players and,
because there are so many servants to manage household problems and
often to take care of small children, wealthy women often play bridge
during the day. Games may continue into mid- afternoon or until the
hour for tea. Tea parties are popular and hostesses display their
best china and silver to guests who make a point of dressing elegantly
for these affairs.

Later, toward the evening, there are cocktail parties in homes and
sometimes these are followed by a buffet dinner or both may be given
in a country club. Gardens are used when the weather is dry and lawns
are green.

San Jose has an active social life and a visitor who is fortunate
enough to be invited to participate in the activities will have an
excellent opportunity to meet people under especially pleasant
circumstances.

Sports which are popular include tennis, hunting, fishing and boating.
Boating however, is done in the hot coastal towns which may be
uncomfortable for someone unaccustomed to such a climate.

When a guest is invited for dinner he or she may arrive on time or
about five minutes early. It is not customary to bring a present.
The host or hostess will probably open the door to greet a guest and
escort him or her to the salon or living room. Here wine or cocktails
are served, but seldom are they accompanied by hors d'oeuvres. Within
about fifteen minutes all will go to the dining room, the oldest son,
father or mother leading the way. The dining table will have a cloth

and cloth napkins and silverware such as that in Europe or the United States. The host will sit at the head of the table and the hostess at the opposite end, the guests at the sides with the honored guest to the right.

Most homes have two places to dine, one in the kitchen and a more formal dining room. However, in many homes there may be only one. In a more traditional or village home, arriving guests will go immediately to the kitchen where everything is very informal and friendly. Drinks will not be served, but the atmosphere is that of one big family. Place mats and paper napkins are often used.

Grace is sometimes said, depending on the family. The guest begins to eat first and children from about the age of six may be a part of the group. Almost all homes have at least one servant. Therefore, one seldom offers to help.

The salad is generally on the table and the meat and vegetables are often passed among the diners. Dinner may consist of a thick soup, such as minestrone, but if there is no soup one starts with the salad, otherwise salad is eaten along with the meal. Salad dressing condiments are vinegar, oil, salt, pepper, and sometimes lemon; each mixes his own. The meat is usually roast beef, sometimes pork, often chicken or fish. These will be accompanied by rice almost always, or sometimes corn kernels which are very large and white. Corn is never served on the cob as it is in the United States. Also used are boiled potatoes with butter and salt, or fried potates. Dessert is often a fruit mixture, "Insalada de fruta," sometimes with ice cream, or cake, or pudding. Ice cream may be on top of jello, which is on top of fresh fruits. Butter is used with bread, but tortillas are popular and often replace bread. Fruit juice is the most popular beverage, and wine and sometimes a stronger whiskey may be used. Ice water is generally served.

The dinner conversation is lively and can cover all subjects. When one is finished eating, the fork and knife are crossed on the plate, prongs down, a spoon may be placed near the top of the plate, face down.

WHEN FINISHED

Coffee is served in the dining room. Guests and hosts leave leisurely and return to the living room, sometimes coffee is offered there, or there may be other beverages offered. You should stay about one half hour at least and from one to two and one half hours after the meal, depending upon the circumstances.

If you wish to thank in Spanish the phrase may be, "Muchas gracias por la comida" and you may always mention how good the food is. No other thanks is expected; no note, no gift, no flowers, no return invitation. In fact, it would be considered strange to invite the family to your hotel for a meal. But, when you leave the country, it is polite to telephone, say goodbye, and mention again the pleasant evening. Then, when you have returned home, a letter or card will be most welcome.

Picadillo de vainicas (string beans minced)

1 pound of ground beef	1 3/4 pounds string beans
1/2 small chopped onion	2 tablespoons oil
1 clove garlic, chopped	1 teaspoon pepper and cumin
4 medium tomatoes, chopped	Salt as desired
1/4 cilantro roll, chopped	2 cups water to cover
(using stems also)	

Wash the string beans, take off the ends, chop in little pieces. Cook the ground beef together with the onion, garlic, tomatoes, cilantro, pepper, cumin, salt and oil. Cook during one half hour until all are mixed. Add the string beans, at a low temperature. Cook for 3/4 hour more with two cups of water. If you need more water, you may add it. Cook until the beans are soft. Serve with white rice. Serves four or five people.

Dulce de durazno (preserve of peaches)

10 sweet peaches	4 cups water
3 cups sugar	2 tablespoons vanilla
3 cinnamon sticks	

Peel the peaches, cook them together with the sugar, cinnamon, water and vanilla until they come to a caramel point.

ECUADOR

Ecuador's capital is Quito, a city on the Pan American Highway, which governs a population of about 40 percent Indian, about 40 percent mestizo, and some Spanish and African. The religion is Catholic and the official language is Spanish, although much Quechua is spoken. Even today, the native Cechua Indians speak their different dialects of this language and have maintained many other living habits and culture of the past. They are colorful people whom visitors see as they drive through the countryside. Although they learned about Christianity and pay their respect to the religion and its Christian God, they have securely held onto their ancient religious beliefs and customs as well.

There are small villages where these Indians still keep to themselves, avoiding Spanish influence. On the other hand, there are white landowners in the secluded highlands who still live in the manner of 18th century Europe with a strong influence of and devotion to their religion which was brought from Spain. Quito, at an altitude of over 9,300 feet and surrounded by hills, is a city of very conservative Catholicism.

In the lowlands near the coast, life is more mixed and modern. Native dances and the original reed pipe music can be seen and heard in the highlands more than in the coastal plains. These are truly traditional and the dances, though colorful, are sometimes quite slow, with stylized movements. You will seldom hear singing.

If you study the topography of Ecuador, you will understand that tradition is easily maintained as it is difficult to communicate and people remain separated from each other. This is a country where a visitor can easily look into the past while seeing its current culture at the same time.

Many people who have not visited the Latin American countries tend to link them together as though they were all the same in culture and climate. Instead, there are differences even when the countries are neighbors. Although the Indians inhabited areas which present boundaries did not divide, after the countries were formed their culture was influenced by those who governed, the economy which developed and the people from other areas of the world who came or were brought to these countries as they were developing. Many of the similarities comes from the original Indian culture which had achieved a high state of civilization and its mark on all of the countries in one form or another.

Ecuador has been a Republic since 1822. There is vast geographical variation from the coast to the Sierra or highlands, and the Orient or eastern jungle. The Galapagos Islands are also a part of Ecuador. Climate varies according to area. Rule was Inca, Spanish, and in more recent years a series of Presidents, most of whom did not finish one term. There has been political turbulence, but the citizenry is warm and friendly.

Usually people eat dinner about 8 p.m. You probably would be invited for 7:30 p.m. and you should arrive on time. It is not customary to bring a gift or flowers.

The person who invites the guest usually will greet you at the door and lead you to the salon or living room where some wine or vermouth may be served. Within about one half hour the same person will escort the guests to the dining room. The dining table will be covered with a cloth, often white but sometimes colored, napkins, the customary silverware. The host sits at the head of the table and hostess often sits at his side, but this depends upon the family.

Some families say Grace and some do not. It would be wise to be ready for it before beginning a conversation. The person who invited the guest will imply when it is time for him or her to begin to eat, as the guest begins first.

There will be wine, fruit juices, or water and the dinner will consist of soup, salad, with lemon and oil dressing which has been pre-mixed, meat (beef, chicken, pork or fish), always rice steamed or in a casserole, sometimes potatoes, bread, with no butter, jello, pudding, or fruit salad. Sometimes coffee is served.

Conversation is plentiful and covers all subjects. One may offer to help if there is no servant.

It is polite to stay about one hour or more after the meal, depending upon the circumstances. Thanks is offered when saying goodbye, the hosts may be invited to your hotel for a dinner or lunch. Flowers or a note may be sent but this is not customary. When leaving the country it is polite to telephone and say goodbye. If it is with a close friend, a letter from your home may be expected, otherwise this is not necessary.

Dishes in Ecuador differ from place to place, mainly because of the topography and the difference in climates.

Caldo de bolas de verde (platano verde: green plantain)

4 green plantains	Pepper
Beef with the bone (like soup meat)	Onions

2 eggs   Tomatoes
Raisins   Green Pepper
Salt

Cook plantain, peel and cut in two pieces, boil in salted water. Put
in fork to see when soft but do not over cook as it will fall apart.
Fry the chopped onions, green pepper and tomatoes then put them and
the meat in salted water and cook until meat is soft. Now mash the
plantain which have been removed from the water until they are like a
stiff dough, not too smooth. Boil the eggs and peel and cube them.
Remove the meat from the pot and cut in little pieces, mix the meat
and eggs and raisins. Make balls about two inches round and hollow
inside and stuff them with all the above mixture; cover well with the
plaintain dough.   Then put the balls back into the soup broth and
boil. When they are very hot they are ready to serve. Sometimes some
chopped peanuts are added to the mix. Serves 6 people.

Platano (plantan, ripe, or yellow)

Slice the plantains longway in half. Fill with a mild cheese, can be
Monterey Jack. Cover with a batter of eggs, flour, water and salt.
Fry in oil in a frying pan until golden.

EGYPT

With one of the longest continuous recorded histories of any city, Cairo, the capital of Egypt, has a museum of the treasures of the kings which interests all visitors. A civilization of highest quality, its pyramids still standing and majestic, one seems to be in the past while realizing that the modern is contrasting that past at every turn. Except for the water of the Nile, the country is barren and dry. The weather is warm and arid and most of the people live near the river and its delta. The Suez Canal has been a cause for friction and sometimes domination.

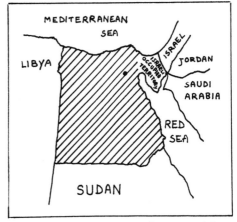

Egypt was declared a Repujlic in 1953 and since has attempted to unify the Arab counties. A visitor will find items to buy from beads to camel saddles, and the buying itself can be an interesting experience. In many shops and business offices you will be offered the traditional coffee served in tiny delicate and decorative containers. You should always accept at least one cup of coffee, although a visitor who has not developed a taste for truly strong coffee many not enjoy it at all. If you are fortunate enough to like the taste, you certainly will not only relish it, but you will please your host very much. It will help you to enjoy Egypt as a whole as the coffee is delicious and the friendship which accompanies it should make you feel welcome. Shopping is an art and you should take time, look at many items, and always bargain when you can.

Entertainment will often include belly-dancing which is a special form of graceful art. The simpler dancing that is seen in many western countries seldom compares with that of Egypt where it has been perfected and is appreciated by the general populace and where the muscle control is studied and practiced for years by the best dancers. Dancers need not be young and some of the older ones have been the most admired. The rythmn of the music lends itself perfectly to this type of dancing and you will remember a performance with pleasure after you have seen one in Egypt, especially in Cairo, where the best are anxious to perform.

Time, to the Egyptians, has a different meaning than in the United States and greater value is put on it in negotiating or trading. It is written in the Koran that "Haste is of the Devil". Traditionally, one is expected to give much time to a friend who might need it. Sharing with friends is totally expected but friends are not made quickly as a rule. They are developed carefully and then a binding trust builds between them which is demonstrated in any time of need. Egyptians do not like to rush through their days, but take the time to enjoy or pursue what is done. This philosophy stems from past cultural patterns and even though their cities may be very modern, their mode of living has an inner calmness about it. Egyptians are proud of their heritage and customs which they blend into modern living.

Unusual for this part of the world near the Mediterranean, is the habit of eating large breakfasts. As a visitor you may be surprised by the many varieties of foods which are eaten at this time of the day. After this, and between lunch and dinner, many small items such as dates and figs, soft drinks and tea and coffee are consumed. Sheep, often mutton, may be the favorite meat and you may find this too rich if you are unaccustomed to it. However, other meats such as chicken are plentiful along with fish. Desserts are abundant and can be very sweet. If you like Egyptian foods and the local hospitality - beware of the calories.

Instead of being invited for dinner one is usually invited to the mid-day meal which is the main meal in Egypt. Lunch will be at about two to four in the afternoon and you will be invited for the day. A good time to arrive will be at 11 or 12 o'clock. You may bring a gift, cake or candy for the children. Flowers are only brought if someone is sick, or for a wedding. The host or oldest son will greet and escort you to the special guest room which has two doors, one which opens to the outside of the other which opens into the house. It is customary to look around the house. The lower floor will be for the family and the upper floor for the married sons and their families. There is a traditional and a modern setting. In the modern there will be western type furniture, sofas and chairs. In the traditional there will be a high wooden bench built against the wall as a bed, or you may sit on the floor.

Hands are always washed before and after eating, either in a bowl or in a bath room. There will be soap and a towel if the water to wash is in the dining room. There may be knives at the table in a modern home, but not in the traditional. Bread is flat and food is often put into it. It is also used to pick up food while eating.

The hostess and host will usually sit together and children above the age of six may join the group. There will be a cloth and napkins. No prayer is said before eating. You may be asked if you prefer a fork, knife and spoon, but it will please your hosts if you eat as they do. Unless there is a maid you may offer to help although you may be thanked and denied.

All the food will be placed in the center of the table and there may be chicken, lamb, duck, macaroni, ochre, salad, pickles, soup (for this you will use a spoon), boiled small egg-plant split into halves and served in the shell and flavored with garlic, cumin, hot pepper and lemon juice. This last is to promote the appetite. After the meal and after washing hands, all return to the guest room for dessert, tea, baklava or kenafa, which are light, crisp, delicate sweets. Most desserts when made abroad are heavier and one should taste them in Egypt to realize their true flavor.

Conversation may cover any subject and you may compliment the food and ask for a recipe if you wish. You will be urged to eat more and you may have to be politely firm if you cannot manage all that is offered. Egyptians always ask you to stay longer saying it is too early to leave. Here you must be firm. A good time to leave might be at six, seven, or at the latest nine in the evening.

You may thank at the door and you may send a note or a gift, although this is not necessary. Do not invite your hosts to your hotel to reciprocate. A letter from your home later will be appreciated.

FINLAND

Located between the 60th and 70th parallels of latitude, Finland is the country farthest north on the European continent. Helsinki is the capital of this nation which has about one third of its territory in the Arctic Circle. Lakes and forests abound, but its climate is tempered by the Gulf Stream and the water of its over 60,000 lakes. Finnish is the native tongue and most of the people belong to the Evangelical Lutheran Church. The other ethnic groups making up the population are Lapps, Jews, Russians, Gypsies and Tatars, but these are a very small 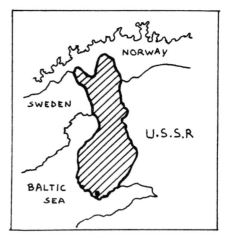 percentage of the whole. A kingdom rule began about 1150 and cooperation between Sweden and Finland was continous. Later, there was a declaration of independence and a bitter civil war. A fierce conflict took place during World War II with Russia, with whom a peace treaty has been signed. Finland is now a constitutional republic with a parliamentary form of government.

There is an old Finnish story which describes the people's attitude toward others: "There were two brothers who had separated during a war. After many years they located each other again and, discovering both were alive, decided to have a reunion. They decided to meet in a certain room, in a certain restaurant at a certain time. After they ordered, the waiter placed a bottle of vodka on the table with two glasses. The two filled their glasses, one lifted his and gave a toast, 'Kippas'. The other brother looked at him and said, 'Did we come here to drink or to talk?'" This may be a tale, but it reflects the fact that Finns are not spontaneously open to strangers and even friends at times. They are pleasant, but keep to themselves, perhaps because they have learned through the war years not to trust others too readily.

The art of cooking is considered very important in Finland and the chefs in restaurants and hotels are very versatile. Fish dishes are popular and plentiful because of the vast water areas, but meats are also a main part of the diet and because of the climate and geographical location of Finland, reindeer meat is a normal dish.

Most Finns eat dinner about seven o'clock. Guests should arrive on time and they may bring flowers, gifts or candy. The host usually greets the guest at the door saying, "Tervey tulula" (with health we welcome you). Then all sit together in the salon or living room for about one half hour. Coffee, cookies, and cakes are usually served and sometimes there will be strong drinks. These are usually unmixed and one should realize their strength; no mixed cocktails are used.

If you are a very close friend you will probably be invited to have a sauna before eating. The women will go first to a room in another part of the house, in the cellar, or out of the house; the men will take their saunas later while the women are preparing the food. Finns do not mind bathing together, but if you are not a very close friend, you may not be invited to take the sauna. During the cooling off period, after the sauna, there will be about one half hour for drinks, often soda and beer. This may be in a rest area close to the sauna.

At the table the host will begin to eat when all are seated and he will give the same toast as when he greeted the guests at the door. The hostess will toast each guest but no one can toast her; the others can toast everyone else.

Finnish formality is similar to Sweden. Usually the group will sit for a long time at the table. The table will have a white linen cloth and napkins, usually china, silver and sometimes there will be a brightly colored paper cloth with matching napkins, especially in a more modern setting. The host sits at one end, the hostess at the other and the guests sit at the sides, men on one side, women on the other facing them. There may be children of any age in the group. The women serve and clean the dishes, but one should not offer to help unless this is a truly modern family. Some will say grace before the meal begins.

The fork is held in the left hand; when finished the silver may be left in any position on the plate. Never use fingers for eating, even with fruits.

Dinner may consist of a salad with cucumber, tomato, lettuce and a small amount of dressing of vinegar and oil; cheese, hard bread and butter; meat (often pork chops for guests), fish, raw or cooked, with sauce; potatoes, carrots, other vegetables; dessert, such as rice cakes or pudding, fruit soup, "kukkula", pastry, ice creams. A berry base, raisins, or prunes, in a thick syrup, served hot or cold, is the fruit soup. Beverages are milk, water and sometimes wine. There is not a great deal of talk during meals as the people are often not very communicative. One may compliment and express thanks for the food.

When the group returns to the living room pastries and candies are sometimes served. One should remain from one half hour to about two hours depending upon the circumstances. In the winter much coffee is drunk. In the summer there may be a barbecue outside and the food may be cooked over the sauna heater.

After a guest leaves he does not send flowers or a gift and probably would not invite the family to his hotel to thank his hosts. However, it is important to telephone the next day or call in person; do not send a note. Finns are very hospitable when you know them but they may seem reserved as was stated in the folk tale. They may not show their emotions as much as some other Europeans. Do not be offended if they do not seem too anxious about your visit. In reality you are truly welcome.

Kalakukko (fish pie)

2 cups water
1/2 cup melted butter
3 1/2 cups rye flour
3 cups white flour
2 teaspoons salt
pinch of pepper
1/4 lb. thin slices of bacon

In a large bowl mix;
3 cups rye flour
1/2 cup butter
1 1/2 cups white flour
1 teaspoon salt

Add more white flour if needed to make a nice dough. Now put the dough on a board which has a little flour on it and knead until it feels smooth. Roll this into a large oval shape 1/2 inch thick, 18 inches long and 12 inches wide. Sprinkle a little rye flour on this.

Rinse and drain the fish on paper towels; then mix 1/2 cup rye flour, one teaspoon salt, and pepper. Toss fish in this in a paper bag. Now lay the fish pieces evenly on the center of the dough in a rectangle or circle shape and put the bacon pieces on top, leaving a good portion of the dough uncovered. Pull the sides of the dough up over the fish covering it all and seal the edges shut using a little touch of water if needed. Put the pie on a baking sheet with the sealed side down. Brush melted butter over it. Bake for 4 hours in a 300° oven and repeat the brushing with butter now and then. When it is served, cut a hole in the top and scoop out the fish. Break off pieces of the crust to eat with it. This is about enough for 12 small servings.

Kaljakeitto (beer soup)

2 tablespoons flour
1 tablespoon sugar
pinch of salt
1/2 teaspoon ground ginger

2 cups milk
1 cup beer
1 tablespoon dark corn syrup
1 cup diced Swiss cheese

Mix: flour, milk, sugar, salt in small pan and heat while stirring until it boils; then continue cooking for one minute more. Turn off heat and cover pan.
Mix: beer, syrup, and ginger in another pan and heat while stirring

until it boils.   Take it off the fire and stir into it the milk
mixture. Heat again to boiling point. Put cheese into bowls and pour
soup over it. Serve very hot!

Paronpaisti (Reindeer meat)

If you do not like the wild flavor of reindeer meat you may soak
it in beer or butter-milk; or you may cook it without soaking.

1 pound bacon
2 pounds reindeer meat
 cut in paper thin slices
1 teaspoon salt

Brown the bacon in a large frying pan and add the meat slices. Over a
high flame, sear the meat quickly; when all the meat is brown,
sprinkle with the salt and lower the flame. Add enough water to cover
the meat. Cover the pan and simmer slowly for 20 minutes. Serve hot
--to about 6 or 8 people.

FRANCE

Paris, the capital of France, is one of
the best known cities of the world to
tourists, and known to all as a city of
beautiful architecture. Ethnically the
French groups are Celtic, Latin and
Teutonic. The religion is Roman
Catholic. A monarchy existed until the
French revolution of 1789, which
established a republic based upon some
of the American ideas of government.
Historically France has been a major
power in world trade and politics. The
climate is generally one of mild summers
and cool winters. French is the
official language and it sometimes is so
jealously guarded that visitors may find that their unperfect accents
difficult for a native to accept. One should not be discouraged about
using the language, however, especially in the more rural areas where
it will be accepted with a friendly hospitality.

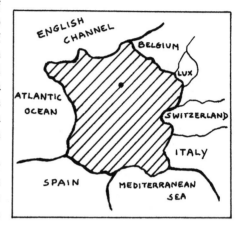

French wines should be enjoyed by all who visit this country where
vineyards cover much of the agricultural territory. In the 19th
century the wine industry was a flourishing part of the French
economy, but in 1880 there appeared a dreaded plague -- a blight
which, it developed, only could be cured by drowning. This meant that
the vines would have to be covered with water for a certain period of
time. A few were saved by this method but it is obvious that since
grapes are not planted in basins, it was almost impossible to cover
most with water. At the same time, the grapes of California had begun
to prove their strength. These vines were started from cuttings of
Mission grapes, or the plants brought by the Spanish missionaries when
they came north from Mexico. Rootings from this hardy strain were
brought to France where the national cuttings were grafted to them,
thus producing the same famous French grapes on the California root
stock. The plague, known as phylloxera, was wiped out and the wine
industry regained its former position of importance.

It is well to read about French wines and to learn where to sample the
various varieties before your visit. Wine tasting tours are popular
and, as in most wine areas of the world, the best food and wine
combinations are those which you may find in the specific areas where
vineyards are cultivated.

French cuisine is internationally known and dishes are delightfully
prepared. The dinner hour begins about eight in the evening or
later. One may arrive five or ten minutes late, but the most polite
person will arrive on time. For an eight o'clock meal you may be

invited at seven. A gift such as flowers, pastries, wine, champagne, candies or a plant may be brought by the guest. The hostess or any family member, or a servant, may greet you at the door and escort you to the salon where you will spend about one half hour while cocktails are served. Whiskey, vermouth, Dubonnet, or other drinks may be offered but usually the mixed cocktails, such as are served in the United States, will not be served. There will be hors d'doeuvres to accompany the beverages. The hostess will announce that dinner is served and the host will escort all to the table, where he will sit at the head of the table. The hostess sits at the other end, which is usually closest to the kitchen, the guests at the sides, and as much as is possible, men and women are alternated. There will usually be a white table cloth and napkins--paper napkins are not used.

Before beginning a meal most people will say "Bon appetit", which means, "I hope you have a good appetite". The hostess then often begins eating first. The dinner will probably consist of soup (especially in winter) followed by pate (charcuterie), to which guests serve themselves. This pate of various types is eaten with bread and butter and red wine. The main course may be meat with red wine, fish with white wine, or fowl with rose or a light red wine. Sometimes meat and fish will be served at the same meal. There will always be vegetables, and bread will be available from soup to dessert. Salad may have pre-mixed vinegar and oil dressing. Cheese is almost always served, and dessert may be fresh fruits, cooked fruits, or pastries.

You may compliment the food. The French are proud of their cooking and will be happy when it is appreciated. Conversation may be abundant and about any subject. When one has finished eating, the fork and knife should be left crossed on the plate, fork prongs down.

NOT FINISHED   WHEN FINISHED

As in China, some foods such as escargot (snails) were originally used when food was scarce and since have become a delicacy. The French sauces are famous and their delicate flavorings grow more pleasant as one tries more dishes. Foods are not strong or hotly spiced and pastries are usually light and airy. French bread is excellent.

Coffee will be served in the salon and will be accompanied by liqueur. Here you should stay for at least one half hour and leave when you think the conversation is ending, using your judgment.

Guests may invite their hosts to a meal at their hotel or a restaurant, but it is not expected that you do so. A thank you note and a letter from your home when you have returned telling them about your travels and inviting them to visit will be appreciated.

Quiche Lorraine

2 cups flour
Almost 3/4 cup butter
1 egg
1 1/2 tablespoon cold water
1/2 teaspoon salt

Mix flour, sliced butter and salt in a mixer until butter is almost
smooth; add egg and 1/2 of water and mix until dough becomes a ball
(you can add more water if needed). Put in refrigerator for about 30
minutes or more. Roll out for a pie crust of two pieces of nine
inches each. Makes two uncovered pies.

Filling:
Cook, drain and chop 4 strips of bacon
1/4 teaspoon white pepper
1/4 teaspoon nutmeg
1/2 teaspoon salt
1 1/2 cups cream
Swiss cheese (about 4 ounces)
3 whole eggs
Grate cheese in large-hole grater

Mix eggs, salt, pepper, nutmeg and cream together. Bake the pie
crust in hot (about 450°) oven for up to 10 minutes, being sure it
does not burn. Put into the pie crust the bacon and cheese but save a
little cheese for the top. Then add the mixture of cream, etc., over
it and sprinkle the rest of the cheese on top. Bake about 45 minutes
until top puffs up and is a little browned. Serve hot. This is a
good dish for a luncheon or served before a meal.

Coq au Vin

1 small chicken cut into small pieces
12 to 15 small white onions...(little round ones)
6 slices of bacon also cut in small pieces
Clove of garlic, cut very fine or put through garlic masher
A pinch of thyme (fresh if possible) and same amount of dill,
Salt and pepper.
1 bay leaf
Parsley to taste (chopped)
1 large cup of beef broth or 1 can of broth
1 1/2 cups of white wine
Fry the bacon and keep the fat separately
In the fat, fry the onions and garlic and drain
Put chicken pieces in a paper bag with a little salt, pepper and flour
or very, very fine bread crumbs and shake until the pieces are
covered. Brown chicken pieces in the same fat from the bacon after
taking out the onions, then add the wine and the other ingredients
back to the pan and cook very slowly, covered, until the chicken is

tan colored and tender. If you wish, you may add some fresh mushrooms
to the mixture, cut in slices. Serve hot.

GERMANY (FEDERAL REPUBLIC OF GERMANY)

Bonn, a university city on the Rhine and
the birthplace of Beethoven, is the pro-
visional capital of the Federal Republic
of Germany.   This government began in
the post World War II period. But the
history preceding these years is filled
with   political,   social   and   warring
contacts with other countries of Europe,
and   with   industrial developments which
were   to   affect   the   world such as the
production   of   toys,   fine instruments,
motors   and   lenses   as   well as techno-
logical   advances   in   the   sciences,
medicine,   music   and   many others. The
Germans   have been an energetic people

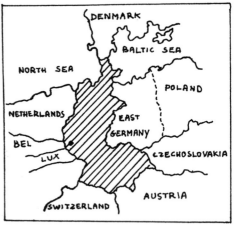

and more   than once have followed their leaders with full force. The
population   consists   of   Germans,   Danes,   and   many recent immigrant
workers   from   Greece,   Turkey,   Italy and Yugoslavia. Protestant and
Roman   Catholic   are   the   two main religions. German is the official
language.

As you travel through the country you will find that the food varies.
Sauerbraten   is   a very popular dish which has, as its name implies, a
sour   taste.   It consists of meat cooked with vinegar and you may have
to   become   accustomed   to this taste before you will enjoy it. It is
found   in all the areas of Germany. Weisswurst, on the other hand, is
usually   found   in the south. This is a white sausage which is boiled
instead of cooked in barbecue fashion.

Beer   parlors   are   especially   popular   with   young Germans. Beer is
served in varying size mugs or glasses. The usual serving is one half
liter,   but in the south you may ask for "ein mass bier" which will be
a   full   liter.   The waitresses have developed strong muscles and can
carry   up to ten full liter mugs at one time while serving. Sometimes
there   will   be   light   snacks such as sausages or sandwiches to enjoy
with   your   beer.   Many people will be playing card games: "skat" in
the   north,   played   by groups of three and "dobbelbock" in the south,
played   by   four.   Usually   they   play for rounds of beer, the loser
buying.   There will be some small tables where the card players often
sit but most tables are long and narrow.

You   may   find,   especially   if   there   is   a   large   group, that very
informally   the   people   will   begin to sing a song and the whole room
may   join   in.   If you know the song, by all means sing with them as
they   will   enjoy it, but if you do not, you may just listen and enjoy
their   enthusiasm.   Usually   beer   parlors are open from about eleven
o'clock in the morning until two the next morning.

The evening meal may be very simple with cold meat cuts, sausage, cheeses, bread and usually served with beer, whereas the meal at noon is often the one to which a guest may be invited. People often do not even sit together to eat, but may get some bread and a bit of sausage and eat it whenever they feel a little hungry; in fact, the evening snack is sometimes not eaten at all. This is just opposite to the custom in America of having the main meal in the evening.

In restaurants people do not ask for water. If you were to request a glass the owner would assume that you are too poor to buy beer or wine and they would wonder why you do not order those customary beverages. You should also be sure not to eat with your fingers, such foods as pizza, fried chicken or corn on the cob are acceptable in America, but in Germany, as in other European countries this would be considered very crude. A fork and knife is used for all such foods including fresh fruits.

Lunch in Bavaria may be served from twelve to one o'clock, in northern Germany it may be later depending upon the children in the family and their school hours; often lunch will begin at two in the afternoon. One may arrive about five or ten minutes after the time of the invitation. Flowers, candy, or a bottle of wine may be brought to your host if you desire. The host and hostess will usually greet you at the door and escort you to the salon or living room where some sherry, whiskey, vermouth, or another aperitif will be served. However, seldom will beverages stronger than beer or wine be served. Occasionally, if the guests are from America or England, they may be offered a cocktail, but even this is unusual. Usually there will be no hors d'oeuvres. This will take about twenty minutes or one half hour, after which time all will go to the dining room. The table will probably be oblong, with a cloth which may be colored, napkins may be cloth or paper. Seating may be informal and may change from time to time; sometimes couples may sit together, sometimes men will face each other, but you will be told where to sit. There are two phrases which may be said before eating: "Gesegnete Mahlzeit" (Have a blessed meal), or "Guten apetite" (Good appetite). Some families say Grace.

The food will usually be on the table; the hostess may start to pass dishes around and all help themselves. Meals may begin with a simple dish of shrimp cocktail, salmon, or trout, then a second dish may be passed or served later by the hostess or a daughter. There is generally fresh salad and sometimes there will be no cooked vegetables as the salad will take their place. Orange juice, wine, beer or milk may be the beverages, but seldom water. Beef or pork or veal or chicken are common, pork being very popular. Bread is not always served, but potatoes, especially boiled, cut and salted are common. Sometimes there may be rice or noodles or "Knodel". (This is raw potatoes and boiled potates mixed to equal a dough; boil in round balls and use meat sauce on this.) Potatoes or cauliflower are often served with a white sauce and meat balls of pork or beef may have a white sauce also.Dessert may sometimes be cake, ice cream, or pudding, or knodel can be filled with plums and served with cinnamon and sugar or with a type of cheese similar to cottage cheese, but a little more like yogurt. This same cheese may be served with fruits for dessert.

The conversation may be about any subject and will continue throughout the meal. One may compliment the food and ask for a recipe, or offer to help.

Coffee is served after a lunch and after evening meals there may be wines. One should stay from one half hour to one and one half hours after lunch and one half hour to two or three hours after dinner.

You may express your thanks while saying goodbye. You may also call again to thank your hosts, and you may send flowers if you have not brought them another gift when you came for the meal. But in any event, you should write when you return to your home and thank them again, telling about your travels and extend an invitation for them to visit you.

GHANA

Ghana is situated only a few degrees from the equator. Accra, its capital, is one of the African cities from which slaves were shipped to other areas of the world. The climate varies according to the geographical areas and may be hot and dry or humid and warm with two rainfall seasons. Most believe that people migrated to this area from the Volta River and other sections further north. Ghanaians speak more than fifty languages or dialects but English is the official language. Ghana's religions are Animist, Christian and Muslim. The country used to be known as the Gold

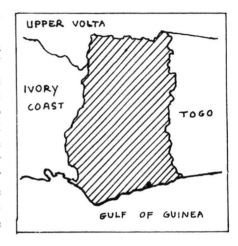

Coast and its history goes back many centuries, but much of it preserved only through folk tales. Rule has been Portuguese, English, Danish, Dutch and German, if not in total area, in the coastal sections of the country. In 1957 Ghana became an independent state. The government has seen internal turmoil but the people are individually friendly and hospitable.

The market places are very colorful in Ghana. You can shop for cloth by walking on dirt roads through a myriad of bundles of brilliantly colored cottons of endless designs. It is tempting to buy yardage of each design as all are beautiful. The market is filled with people and the clothing they wear is made of the same colorful materials. All items are displayed by their vendors and there seems to be action everywhere.

Bread is often sold along the roadways. If you walk near these stalls you will be enticed by the aroma of fresh hot loaves of delicious bread and you will never tire of its taste. The people of Ghana are excellent bakers and they are eager for you to enjoy their products.

Dinners may be from four in the afternoon to six in the evening. If a guest arrives later, the family may already have eaten and they will fix the food for him separately, depending upon when he or she drops in. This is due to the "extended family" system of society and whoever drops in is offered food at that time. One is invited to "supper" not to dinner, and no time may be given. An invitation might be, "Would you mind dining at my house today?". You may arrive at any time after three o'clock. Another reason for this is the transportation problem.

You may bring a gift, something small from your native country, or flowers. The host will greet you at the door and lead you to a living room where the furniture is western style. The greeting will be

"Akwaaba" (You are welcome). You will be given some water during which time everyone welcomes you, then you are offered what you wish to drink: coke, soft drinks, beer, hard drinks, whiskey, schnapps or other drinks. A variety is usually offered. There will be no hors d'oeuvres except during Christmas when special tiny biscuits, about the size of a nickel, are served and there may be a cake. Guests stay here about one half hour up to three hours depending upon the circumstances. There will be a bowl to wash your hands in the same room, and the meal will be eaten in this same room, an adjacent alcove, or a separate dining room.

Christians usually say Grace, others, depending upon their religion, will say a prayer and some will say nothing. Sometimes very young children will join the group. There will be a table cloth and cloth napkins. The host will sit at one end and the hostess at the other or near the host, guests at the side; seating is informal. The beverage during the meal will likely be water. Soup and the main dish and salad are all served simultaneously. There may be "Fu fu", plantain and cassava mashed like mashed potatoes, or "Kenkey", a corn dough about the consistancy of a tamale; this is served with stew. The stew is made of tomato paste, pepper, onion, spices, meat, and fish. Rice may also be served with stew. "Jolly Rice" is rice with stew. Salad will have an oil and vinegar dressing pre-mixed or mixed individually. "Ampesi" is either yam or plantain or coca yam with "Pallava" sauce, which is spinach pureed with pieces of meat. "Banku" is like Kenkey but without the cornhusk. There are a variety of dishes which vary according to the regions. After the main dish there will be tea or coffee or another drink offered and you will be asked if you wish something else, such as fruit or pudding.

Conversation is sparse at meals, although you may compliment the food and offer to help the hostess, but probably you will not be able to do it, especially in homes with a servant.

People in Ghana eat quickly and you should try to do the same in order to finish at about the time they are through. Usually ages are grouped together, such as the children in one group, elderly in another. Everyone eats from the same dish and you should eat from your side of it, never reach across the dish to help yourself.

When you eat the fish you may find it difficult to chew. This is known as "stock" fish and is so hard it must be cut with a saw or electric knife. It is the fish most used in dishes and it has the consistency of rubber when chewed. Do not try to hurry this chewing process as it will do you no good, it simply takes a long time. Fu Fu is eaten with the fingers using the right hand only.

At the end of the meal, hands are again washed in a fresh bowl of water in the dining area. Soap and towels will be offered as the food is often eaten with the fingers, although some may use a fork. This

depends upon the foods. Fingers are used for Fu Fu, Kenkey and Banku.
Rice and other dishes may be eaten with a fork. Sliced avocados may
be used as a vegetable.

Usually all the food will be on the table and you will help yourself
starting at any time after Grace is said. Guests may be specially
served by some hosts. After dinner, one should stay at least a half
hour.   You may be invited to spend the night and you must use your
judgment about how long to stay as each case will be different. The
after dinner hour is the time for talk and tea, bread and milk, or
ovaltine, milo, but seldom will hard drinks be served.

Thank you has a singular and plural: "Me dawo ase", singular; "Me
damo ase", plural; and "Me pese me ko" is goodbye.

You can write a note, send flowers, but do not invite your hosts for a
meal. They really prefer you to do nothing as they wish to do all for
you.   Do telephone when leaving the country, and expect that some of
them may come to see you off. A letter from your home after you have
returned is appreciated.

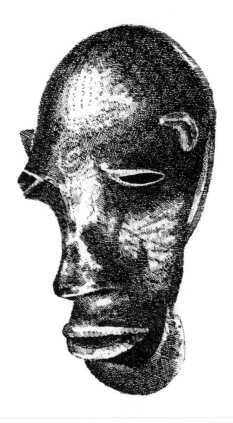

HAITI

Haiti, a part of an island in the Caribbean Sea, has as its capital Port-au-Prince. It is a republic with only about one third of its land suitable for cultivation. It is in the tropics and the weather is warm to hot and humid in many areas. Haiti has one of the world's most dense populations made up of about 95 percent of African descent and the others are mixed descent, Europeans, or Levantine descent. French is the official language but many speak Creole. All religions are recognized but the official one is Roman Catholic, although there is much voodoo practiced.

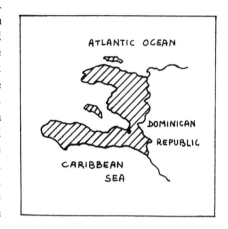

The island was discovered by Columbus in 1492 and since then it has had a history of piracy or harassment by the English and Spanish ships. Later on agriculture flourished and the island became rich, many slaves having been imported to work on the sugar and coffee plantations. In 1804 the slaves established their independence and named the country Haiti. There have been many dictators and much political turmoil and there was an United States occupation which ceased in 1934. Haiti now has a constitution and a president.

Here the meal to which you may be invited will probably be at noon. You may arrive from ten minutes early to ten minutes after the invited hour. In some families the French custom is followed and dinner will be about 6:30 in the evening. Arrival time will be the same. There will probably be a maid who will greet and escort you to the foyer, where you may sit for about five minutes. Then the hostess will arrive and invite you to the salon or living room where wine, Dubonnet, or French type drinks will be served, which may be accompanied with croissants. Time spent here is usually about 15 to 20 minutes. Hands are washed 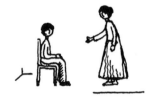 in the rest or powder room on the way to the dining room. The dining table is usually oblong and the seating arrangements depend upon the family. Children usually eat with the group unless they are very small. Cutlery and cloth are similar to the French style, though the cloth may be colored. Conversation is pleasant and flowing. The father often offers a blessing and then begins to eat and there will probably be a maid to serve.

A usual meal will have fresh salad with vinegar and oil or mayonnaise dressing, vegetables, which may be fried, plantain with meat (of all kinds) or fish. Bread and butter is used and there will be small plates for this. Dessert may be pudding, cake, or jellied fruits. Wine, milk or juice such as tropical fruit juices may be the beverage. Coffee is served at the table.

When leaving the dining area hands are again washed, and in the living room coffee may again be offered, this time with cookies. One should stay for about one half to one hour after the coffee is served.

"Merci" is the word for thank you and a simple thanks is all that is required; no gift, no note, no flowers. However, it will be appreciated if you call or phone to say goodbye when leaving and invite your host to visit you at home.

Rice and Beans

Kidney beans, boiled, but not over-cooked
Oil in a pan, cotton or soy bean oil, over a low fire
Chives and salt pork

Drain beans and let stand ten minutes, seasoning with salt and pepper and crushed garlic. Add water from beans that were boiling, enough to cover well. Boil for 15 minutes. Wash rice 2 or 3 times, add to boiling water and beans. Add a bouquet of parsley to boil and cover very tightly. Leave until rice is cooked, about 15 minutes (long grain rice is good). For each cup of rice use two cups of water and one cup of beans. Serve hot.

HONDURAS

In Central America, between the Caribbean Sea and the Pacific Ocean, Honduras has a climate which varies from temperate in the mountainous area to tropical in the lowlands, with a dry season which sometimes is long, extending from November to May. Tegucicalpa, its capital, is also the largest city. The population is made up of Caucasians and native Indians, known as Mestizos. Most of the people are Roman Catholic and Spanish is the official language. This area was once a part of the Mayan Empire, later was ruled by Spain through a claim by Columbus. It was also connected with Guatemala during the colonial era. Later it became an independent country with its history marked by revolutions and conflicts with neighbors. The people are friendly and hospitable and they enjoy the beauty of their land.

Hondurans eat their evening meal anytime from 5:30 to 7 p.m. When guests are invited they usually eat at 7 p.m. Guests should arrive at the time invited and not late, especially if there is only one guest. It is not customary to bring a gift or flowers. Usually a son or daughter will greet you at the door and escort you to the salon or living room, where an aperitif which may be wine or brandy will be offered. Hors d'oeuvres are not usually served. The host often leads the conversation and it may be about any subject. Then all will enter the dining room where the host and hostess may sit together at one end of the table with guests at the side and at the other end. If a guest is a close friend of the hostess, she may sit next to her; if they are a couple the host will sit with the visiting lady and the hostess with the visiting husband. Usually all members, sons, daughters and other relatives will be a part of the group. The table will have a cloth and napkins, paper napkins often replacing the cloth ones. The silverware is similar to European or that in the United States.

Usually the host begins and invites all to eat. Grace is not customarily said before a meal. Beverages may be wine or water and always coffee with dinner. Bread and butter is served but little bread plates are not used. Sometimes there will be soup, always rice, and meat, sometimes potatoes, fresh vegetable salad and dessert, which may be cake or fruits of all kinds. Conversation is kept flowing and you may compliment the food. You may offer to help, but your offer will probably not be accepted. After the main meal coffee and dessert are often served in the living room where conversation is light and friendly. Here you should stay from about one hour to about three hours if you are a close friend.

You may send a thank you card, or just thank when leaving, but no gift, and do not invite the hosts to your hotel to reciprocate. But, do write from your home when you have returned and tell about your travels.

Tapado (which means "covered")

2 coconuts
7 green bananas
2 plantain, semi ripe
1 pound chorizo (red pork sausage)
3 pounds smoked ham

1 onion, cut or sliced
Pepper, chili pepper, salt, to taste
2 mashed garlic cloves
2 teaspoons tomato paste or sauce
1 pound yuca (this is the peeled root)

Cut coconut in pieces, dividing it into three parts. Put one section at a time into a blender with 1 1/2 cups warm water each time. Squeeze it through a sieve to get the milk. Let the milk stand for one hour. Put ham to cook in pieces (including the bone; it has a better flavor with the bone) with the garlic, onions, chili pepper and tomato sauce. Cook until tender and then add in a casserole the green bananas in pieces, the plantain, the chorizo and the yuca. Pour the coconut milk over all, add salt and pepper as desired. Cover and cook over a low flame, basting periodically. When the green bananas are tender it is ready to serve.

HONG KONG

Victoria is the capital of the British Crown Colony of Hong Kong which has one of the most picturesque natural harbors in the world. Its weather has a monsoon wind which blows from the north and keeps the country dry and cool and sunny, and a stronger one from the south which brings the heat and rain. The natural coloring is clear and beautiful and one finds many interesting shops. It is easy to feel that all the population of the world is in this place because so many have migrated here. Restaurants, including those on houseboats, are well attended and the food is often delicious. Originally a part of mainland China, Hong Kong was granted to the United Kingdom after the Anglo-Chinese or Opium war. Most of the Chinese here are Buddhists and Taoists with a small Christian group. The language is Cantonese and the official language is English.

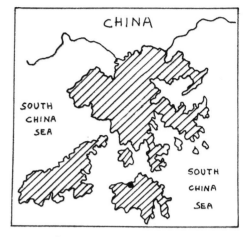

The dinner hour may be about six or seven in the evening. Guests should arrive on time and may bring flowers, a small gift, candies or fruits or cookies, and it is customary to say these are gifts for the children in the family. Fruits are usually brought in a basket and wine, especially if it is imported, may also be brought.

If your host knows in advance the time of your arrival by air, he may meet you at the airport and drive around until near the dinner hour, then take you to the home to talk before dinner. Or, you may be greeted at the door by your hosts or another family member and escorted to the living room which may be separate, or in some instances, a part of the dining area. Tea will be served and there are sometimes some sweets or cookies with it.

Chop sticks and a spoon are used for eating the meal. The food may be placed on the table by the hostess and a servant and it will be in the center where it is easily reached by all. Guests usually sit next to the host. There is no cloth and the table will be highly polished.

Your chop sticks, usually made of ivory, may have written on them, "Wishing all is successful", or for newlyweds "Long life, prosperity", or they may each have half of a saying such as , "Look up and you see the moon" on one, and "Look down and you see your feet!" on the other. The bowl is often held in the hand while eating. Youngsters will often greet the elders by saying, "You eat first", when the young will eat following the elders. Religious families may say Grace and will usually say "Shall we say Grace now?".

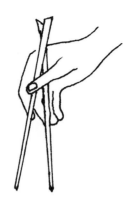

It is wise to practice with chop sticks if you plan to visit countries where they are used. They are held between the thumb, first and second fingers and worked together gently. When one becomes accustomed to this method of eating, he will find it simple and effective.

Tea, wine or soft drinks may be served with a meal and at times, such as when certain types of shrimp foods are eaten, there may be a bowl of tea water to wash hands after eating it. Otherwise, there will be a hot towel offered you after each meal. Do not offer to help, but always compliment the food. The Cantonese word for this is "Doche". Fruit may end the meal and you should stay at least one half hour after it. Thank when saying goodbye; the word of this is "Dzoykin". Do not remain after the meal more than about two hours at maximum unless there is a special reason.

You may invite the hosts to your hotel or restaurant, but it is not necessary. However, do telephone to say goodbye when you are leaving Hong Kong, then write a letter after you have returned to your country.

Chicken and Spring Melon Soup

Ingredients:

1 1/2 pound fresh chicken
8-10 cups water
1 pound spring melon (honeydew, etc.)
8-10 Chinese dried mushrooms

Condiments:

1 tablespoon sherry
1 tablespoon salt
2 slices ginger
1 green onion

Clean chicken; remove skin and seed from melon and cut them into cubes two inches by two inches. Wash mushrooms (with soap); bring water to a boil and add chicken and condiments. Boil in a medium heat for one hour. Add the spring melon cubes and mushrooms and continue to boil for another 30-45 minutes on a medium heat. Serve soup in bowls.

Serves 4 to 6 people. (The chicken will be removed from the soup and can be used in a salad).

HUNGARY

Although located toward the east, Hungary, whose capital is Budapest (actually divided into two sections by the Danube: Buda and Pest) has always been considered by its people to be part of Western Europe. Its religions are Roman Catholic and Protestant. Its language, Hungarian, is one of the most unique languages in the world, being a distant relative of Finnish--sharing a common stem. English and Russian are taught in schools. Except for recent years, Hungary was a monarchy and more recently has been influenced governmentally in varying degrees by Russia, and is now under socialist-communist rule. Roman and earlier ruins are points of interest for a visitor, along with a pastoral scenery and pleasant and gifted people.

In 1475, a marriage between Matthais I, the ruler of Hungary, and Princess Beatrice of Italy, caused great changes in the cuisine of this country. Matthais had already brought the art of cooking into a new era and Beatrice brought one of (or perhaps the) first cook books ever printed along with some famous chefs to her new country. There now began a blend of the old dishes and new tastes, and Hungary, which in these years was a mighty empire, became famous for its elegant and elaborate meals. Recipes have been passed down through the generations and although the meals may not have so many courses as in the past, the individual dishes are as complicated and time consuming to prepare.

Dinners are from approximately seven to eight o'clock and one should arrive on time or no more than five minutes early. It is considered impolite to arrive late. This could be with a group of intellectuals such as lawyers or doctors. You may bring flowers for the hostess, or champagne or wine. The host or hostess may greet you at the door. If, however, you are in the country or a village, you may arrive at an hour or two early for a seven o'clock dinner, as they will state the time they will be eating and will expect you to talk and visit first. Visiting before and after the meal is very important in the rural areas. In these homes you will go directly to the kitchen-main room in old style houses and drinks will be served either there or sometimes in an adjoining bedroom. In the city you will go to a salon

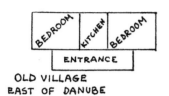

OLD VILLAGE
EAST OF DANUBE

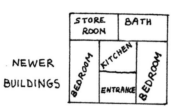

NEWER
BUILDINGS

or living room where there will be wine, coffee, brandy, or schnapps. Conversation at the pre-dinner, dinner and post-dinner time is abundant and can cover all subjects except politics.

After a half hour guests will go into the dining room where the table will probably have a white cloth and napkins. The host or hostess will indicate where to sit or you may sit anywhere, informally. Silverware and dishes are Western style. A toast may be "Servus". Many families may say Grace and all begin to eat simultaneously, often by serving themselves from bowls. The hostess or daughter, or both, often serve and the host only gets up to serve drinks which are not served by the women; usually these are wine or beer. Often everything is on the table and you take what you wish. Dinners may consist of soup, meat, fish, poultry, potatoes, vegetables, mixed dishes, sometimes salad (eaten with the meal), and dessert such as cookies, cake, ice cream, pudding, fruit, etc. Coffee or tea may be offered and sometimes one may mix wine with water. It is customary to compliment the food and female guests may offer to help.

After dinner one may stay from about one half hour until 10 o'clock, or on a Saturday, until 11 p.mm. or 12 midnight, depending upon the circumstances. Sometimes schnapps, wine or coffee and cakes are served after dinner, this being the most social part of the evening.

When leaving, a thank you is sufficient; "Koszonom" (pronounced "Kuzcenum") is the word for thank you. No note is expected, nor phone call, but you may invite your hosts to your hotel for a meal. When you return home you may write to them, but since it may be difficult for them to leave their country, you should not suggest that they visit you.

Toltottkaposzta (Cabbage with stuffed meat)

Cabbage, ground meat, black pepper, paprika, rice, salt, garlic: mixed. You boil the water and put in the cabbage leaves and cook them. When these come to the top, take them out of the water. The mixed meat you roll into the cabbage leaves and put it all back to cook on top of the stove. You have to pour catsup on the rolls and put sauerkraut underneath them. The boiling time for the rolls will be up to one hour.

Crab Salad Raksalata

About 35 to 40 crayfish
4 green peppers, chopped
1 tablespoon grated onion

Dash white pepper, salt,
1/2 teaspoon paprika
1/4 cup olive oil

2 tomatoes, peeled (remove seeds)   3 hardboiled eggs
2 tablespoons tarragon vinegar   1 tablespoon parsley,
                                              chopped

Wash crabs and soak in cold water, change water now and then, for
about 1 1/2 hours; clean each carefully. Boil for about ten minutes,
remove shells, cool them. Boil peppers for short time and mix with
meat of crayfish and tomato. Mix vinegar and salt and paprika and
olive oil. Grate or put the eggs through a sieve and add them to the
vinegar sauce. Put meat in plate and pour dressing over it. You can
put parsley on top to decorate. Serves about 4 people.

INDIA

India is a large, complex country and
foods and customs vary from area to area
and from class to class. New Delhi, the
capital, has a population of about three
million, whereas some other cities have
six or seven million. One often feels
there is too little space for the
people. Hindi and English are the main
languages, although many other Indian
tongues are spoken. The religions are
Hinduism and some Muslim, Christians,
Sikh, Jain, Buddhism and Parsi.
Civilization has been recorded since
2,500 B.C. and contacts with other world
areas have been through trade and
education. Rule has been Aryan, Arab,
Mogul and British and is now
independent.

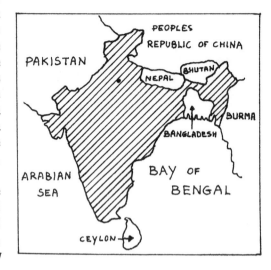

Traditionally men go through a door first and they rise when a lady
enters the room. At meals a man eats first and elderly people sit
first as age must be respected. Many eat more meat and chicken than
they used to, although the cow is still considered to be sacred. A
good Hindu does not eat beef and Muslims do not eat pork, ham or
bacon. People do not enter a kitchen or meditation room wearing shoes
as they may be contaminated and may be made of animal hide. People
wash their hands, legs and rinse their mouths carefully before eating.
Left hands, used for personal cleaning, should never touch a cooking
vessel. All through India the left hand is negative, the right hand
positive. Knives, forks and spoons are used in the cities but
elsewhere may eat with fingers.

Different combinations of curry ingredients develop into different
curry dishes per family, or geographical area, and may be
distinguished as such. Ghee (a form of butter) is used almost as oil
or fat. Sometimes food is eaten from plates but sometimes from banana
or other flat leaves. There may be a strict ritual; at the corner of
the leaf may be placed a pinch of sugar, a piece of fruit and a few
drops of milk which signifies, "Let our friendship be as sweet as
sugar, as filling as fruit, and as wholesome as milk". Guests are
served first. Rice is ladled from a bowl with a spoonlike tool into
the leaf and other items are added, such as lentil custard. Salt
signifies a friendship. Grace is said and some stylized traditional
motions are made to thank for the food. One eats with fingers.
People sit on the floor in loose fitting clothing.

For a more usual type dinner large plates and small bowls are used. Water is the usual drink and there is much buttermilk, yogurt, pudding and soup. Peanuts are used in foods extensively and are fried in rice. Dishes vary from very hot to mild depending upon the families and the regions; there are many spices used in their preparation.

A large portion of Indians do not eat meat, fish or eggs. Except for sweets, there is no special order as everything is served at the same time. A variety of delicious fried cakes (not sweet cakes) may be served at the same meal; these may be flavored with various vegetables. Hot tea in the north and hot coffee in the south are favorites, coffee being served with diluted milk. Cold drinks are popular and may be "ninboo-pani", a lemon drink; "Lassi", beaten yogurt with water; or "Sambaran", the southern version of Lassi, or fresh coconut milk and sugar cane juice. In areas where there is prohibition, no strong drinks will be served.

Eating is an interesting and enjoyable experience in India, but one may not appreciate his first dish or two. Do not be discouraged, try again and you will surely find something palatable within the large range of dishes available.

INDONESIA

An archipelago nation with more than 13,500 islands, Indonesia's capital is Djakarta. It has a tropical climate with more temperate weather in some upland areas. It has a dense population.The people are predominately of Malay stock and speak Indonesian which was derived from Malay. The majority of the population is Muslim with a small number of Christians. The beauty of the islands and the grace of its dancers are world known. Civilization dates back to about 1,000 years before the voyage of Columbus. Rule has been Buddhist kingdom, Hindu kingdom, Islam kingdom, Portuguese and Dutch, with a very brief period of British conflict. The Dutch rule lasted for approximately 350 years and therefore many customs were adopted from its culture. If you hear someone speak of a "Dutch Wife", do not assume that it is a woman. Probably they will be referring to a pillow; one which is shaped like a cylinder or a bolster, and held closely as if hugging it for comfort while sleeping. These are stuffed with kapok (kapuk) which is soft and warming, and produces a cuddly feeling. Often there is no blanket as the weather is warm enough to use the pillow alone. It does not replace what we know as a head pillow. When the Dutch Wife becomes worn and limp, it is ripped open and refilled to regain its fullness. There are architecturally famous temples and buildings from the Hindu period during World War II. Independence was interrupted by Japanese occupation during World War II.

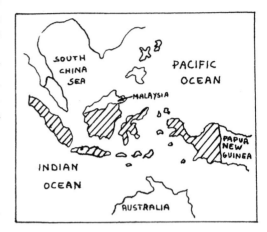

Customs may differ depending upon the religion of a family, but the average family may dine at about 7 or 7:30 p.m. One should arrive at the time invited, a few minutes earlier or later, but the exact moment is preferable.

When you arrive at a private home, before entering it is polite to say "permisi" which means: may I be permitted to enter?

Also, if two or more people are speaking and standing or sitting near each other, anyone who may be serving and entering the room will dip, bending the knees while dropping a hand to his or her side, and say permisi as they walk by.

Guests may bring a cake, or a small snack to serve before or after the meal, but this is not necessary. The pre-dinner visit will last about one half hour in the living room. Because of their religion most families will not have liquor but will serve sweet drinks, a grenadine type punch, or orange juice with snacks. This is a very talkative visit with men and women and the entire family joining in. The hostess, who has prepared the food, will announce dinner and the guests will be told where to sit at the table. The host and hostess may be at one end, the main guests at the other, family members at the sides. You will probably be asked if you wish to drink iced or plain water. The host will ask guests to begin and serve their plates with rice and meats (fish, chicken, beef) cut in small pieces. Pork will not be eaten by Muslim families. The host will say, "Praise to the Lord" before one begins to eat. Spoons are held in the right hand, forks in the left and napkins are left on the table, not on your lap. Left over from the Dutch is the custom, which one may still see, of tucking the napkin in at the neck, but this is not considered the thing to do. There are seldom knives, as foods are usually served in small pieces. A bowl of water for washing your hands will be placed at your right side on the table. When a course is finished the fork

should be left prongs down under the spoon in a crossed position on the plate. If they are left face up it will mean that you have not finished. Spice varies with the regions and Sumatra food is especially hot. Conversation may focus on personal interests. Fruits are served on a second plate and may be eaten with the fingers or a small fork. Bananas and papaya are popular. It is polite to compliment the food and you will please your hosts by doing so.

Upon re-entering the living room you may be offered coffee, but not always. There may be tea or water and snacks while the conversation continues for at least one half hour. It is up to you to judge how long you should stay.

A thank you at the door may include an invitation to your hotel for a meal, if you wish. Thank you is "Terima-kashih", goodnight is "Selamat Malam". Do not send flowers, but you may bring a little gift to say goodbye when you leave the country. If you have not time to call you may send flowers at this time, or a cake or other food and write from your home after you return to invite them to visit.

Sate Sapi is small cubes or chunks of meat skewered and cooked over a fire, then covered with mashed peanuts and catsup sauce.

Gado-Gado is a salad of cooked vegetables such as broccoli, bean sprouts, green beans and cabbage; sliced cucumber, sliced potatoes; hard boiled egg and served under a sauce of mashed peanut base. Foods vary from island to island. For instance, in north Sulawesi the natives eat very hotly spiced dishes. They also enjoy dog meat, rats (which are grown on farms) and large bats.

Most dishes have been influenced by the different ruling governments and eating is a fascinating experience of flavors. Your hosts will be very happy if you try the dishes.

IRAN

Tehran, the capital of Iran, is an old
city which has been modernized and now
resembles most other large cities of the
world.   Much of the country is very
sparsely inhabited as it is mountainous
and desert. The climate is diversified
but summers are hot except in the
highest areas.   The ethnic groups are
Persians, Kurds, Turkomans, Baluchis,
Arabs and some Lur Bakhtiari and Qashqai
tribes.   The religion is Islam with a
few Jews, Christians, Armenians,
Assyrians, Bahais and Zoroastrians.
Persian is the official language.
Iranian night life is filled with music
and many spend hours in a public night
club.

Mosques and bazaars are things to be seen in Iran. The mosques are
decorated with beautiful tiles and intricate designs, but never with
drawings or paintings of figures.   Much of the decoration is
caligraphy, some is of stylized leaves or flowers. The colors are
vivid and often in blue shades. The domes and the nearby minarets
(from where the people are called to prayer) are an architect's
delight.

Bazaars have a completely opposite appeal. They are filled with all
kinds of saleable objects, in every known size, shape and color and
there is constant commotion and noise. It is a time to see friends,
bargain boisterously, and enjoy the whole scene. Originally all the
produce was brought by farmers to a mutually agreed upon and
convenient place on special days to exchange goods. This still
happens in some areas but the usual bazaar now is in a special market
place and is held constantly. There are sections for each type of
merchandise and similar goods are grouped together.   There is
bargaining but money is used and exchanging one product for another is
rare.   There is an excitement about the bazaar that will help you to
understand ancient Iran.

Dinners are from 8 p.m. to 10 p.m. and guests are often invited to
lunch instead of dinner in the evening. Invitations will not be for
cocktails. One may arrive about one hour before the invited time, but
if you are a foreigner and your host thinks you may not know this, he
may tell you to come early. Do not bring a present. The pre-meal
hour can last up to two hours if the group is large. Greetings are
very friendly and there may be much hugging and kissing. Usually the
host will greet you at the door and will escort you to the living room
for the visiting hour. The host will usually lead the conversation,
although more modern families are apt to participate as a whole.

Beverages will vary; pure Persian tradition will call for cokes, lime juice or other cold drinks in the summer and in the winter tea (Chai). Tea is served with cookies, "Kloocheh". The more modern families will ask if you wish a drink, meaning all liquors, Scotch being the most usual. If you decline you will be offered a soft drink with nuts such as cashews, pistaccio and water melon seeds. Fruit may also be offered. When dinner is ready the hostess will announce it. The traditional custom is for all to sit on the floor where a table cloth will be placed. There will be a fork and spoon but no knife--one eats rice with a spoon. There is a "top" and "bottom" of the room and the bottom is near the door. The host sits next to the guests either to the west or east. If it is a group of guests, the oldest sits next to the top. There are no napkins as one washes hands before and after eating. In a more modern home the furniture is western style and all sit at a table. A modern meal may include soup, salad, rice dish and beverage. Beverages may be cokes with ice in glasses and each may have a bottle at his place.

Traditionally hands are washed outside, otherwise, a bowl will be given you; there will be a wash room in the modern house. There will be very little talk with the meal as eating is the important thing. In a modern home, all will go back to the living room where they will be given small plates and a fork and knife. These are for fruit which will be offered and when you have finished the first helping may be offered again. The plates are held on the lap. Kleenex may be offered in place of napkins. Tea is always served after dinner, in holders. Here one may stay and visit for one hour at least before leaving. Always express thanks for the food and say it was good. In the traditional home you may be asked to spend the night, and the host may insist, but you should probably decline. Always make another date while leaving, but a foreigner cannot do this easily, so he may just offer to meet again.

Do not send a present, or a thank you note. When leaving the country always phone to say goodbye. In Iran one must expect that the hosts will insist that you take more, stay longer, etc. You will soon learn what you can accept and how to insist back when you decline.

Salad - Nanoh

Dry or semi-dry mint
Yogurt, about 6 ounces
1/2 cucumber, chopped

4 small green onions
Salt and pepper

Mix and serve very cold.

Chellokabob (Chello-rice, kabob-meat) This is the national dish.

Meat is on skewers, white rice, two kinds of ground meat or chopped lamb, onions and flavorings.

If you are a visitor you will receive an enormous helping of this and when you have finished the hosts will appreciate it if you wish more. Be sure to eat all that you are able of the helping. This may be served with a drink of mixed yogurt and water.

You will find the food more and more enjoyable as you become accustomed to it. But always try it and express appreciation as your hosts will hope that you are enjoying it and will be very happy when you do.

Chello (white fluffy rice)

1 pound or 2 1/4 cups of rice
1/2 butter
1/2 cup hot water
3 lumps of rock salt
Water (cold)

Clean and wash rice thoroughly, cover with lukewarm water and place salt (in a small bag) in it and let remain over night or at least two hours. Bring 7 quarts of water in a large pot to a boil and add one cup of the water in which the rice has been soaked. Remove the foam and drain the rice and sprinkle it gradually into the boiling water. Add one cup of cold water to the boiling rice. Remove the foam occasionally. When the rice grains are tender but not soft, remove from the fire and drain and rinse with lukewarm water. If too salty, rinse again. Melt the butter and add 1/2 cup of hot water to it. Divide this mixture in half and add rice to one half of the butter mixture; cover and place over low heat. After ten minutes remove the lid and insert a knife into the rice. If vapor comes out, pour the remaining half of the butter mixture on the rice and cover with the "Damkoni" a lid made of raffia and encased in a washable removable cover. Cook over very low heat until all the water has been absorbed. Remove from the heat and after two or three minutes remove the Damanki and serve. A layer of rice will remain at the bottom of the pot. Remove it with a spatula and serve. This toasted rice is called "Tah dig" and is a special delicacy.

- 69 -

ISRAEL

Tel Aviv is the generally recognized capital of Israel, although Jerusalem was its proclaimed capital in 1950. Most people know that this new country was formed after the Second World War as a homeland for the Jews. Its population came from various countries around the world and, therefore, foods and customs are diverse. Each Israeli who was interviewed said, "But I can only tell you about my way of living, for I, or my family, came from---country originally and have brought our country's customs and recipes with us." There is a minor population of non-Jews in Israel. The

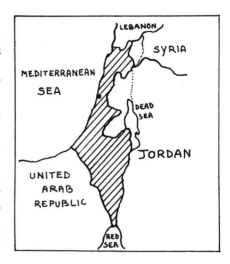

country has seen military strife and peace with neighboring areas is still to be achieved. Summers are mostly hot and dry and winters are mild. City life and rural life differ greatly. The official languages are Hebrew and Arabic, and English is spoken widely.

In Israel, a kibbutz (meaning group) is a collective settlement in which the inhabitants have a particular style of living.

Kibbutzim are cooperative enterprises and set their own patterns according to their members' choice. They plan their own governing rules and choose their governing bodies. The work program is planned and supervised by one group of these governing members. Elected committees are not paid and are rotated in order to give all persons the same opportunities. The general idea is that there shall be equality and no special rulers in a kibbutz.

Usually the kibbutz is in a rural area and was originally formed to help in the development of Israel's economy as a growing country. Work is assigned and this too, is rotated, with members taking such jobs as cultivating, planting, cooking, taking care of living quarters, mending clothes, and the like.

Each member has an equal home, furniture, some money and other necessities and all eat in one main dining room. Although this may vary, it is the usual style for kibbutz life. The children often live in dorms and eat and take their lessons together. Some kibbutzim have joined together for the sake of providing either members with more facilities. Life here is healthy, simple and friendly. A visitor to a kibbutz will find the sharing a unique experience. If you should plan to live in a kibbutz, as some foreigners do for perhaps a few months at a time, you should make careful arrangements in advance which will take into consideration such things as language ability. If you do not speak Hebrew, there are some kibbutzim where English is the spoken language. You will work, play, sing, eat, discuss, and in general become an integral part of the everyday life. This will mean that you must adapt to each segment of the kibbutz philosophy. Many who have shared this experience are completely satisfied and attest to the enjoyment of their stay while others, who may not adapt too readily, should only visit briefly for perhaps a few hours to see and learn what they can about this communal way of living.

A moshav, also a form of group living, resembles a kibbutz with the exception that there is some private management and ownership. These are often more concerned with an industry. Here, each family is more independent and lives in a private home where cooking and house chores are done by the family and children live in the home with their parents. Besides visiting the major cities, you should visit at least one kibbutz in order to understand the different life styles of Israel.

The country, as it is still young, has not yet become unified in its eating customs. The cooking style will vary and resemble the country from which it has been brought. Orthodox families will, of course, have certain rules which are practiced by Jews all over the world. The following is an example of what one might expect of family customs in a medium sized city. Notations are made simultaneously if there is a comparison. A Kibbutz will have one large dining room where everyone eats together; a Mochav Shitufi is like a cooperative and a Mochav Ovdim is similar but people have individual properties and these families eat in their different homes. There are customs which have their origins in Europe and those which will relate more to such North Africa areas as Morocco, Tunis, Algeria, or Lybia. All eat with silverware such as is used in Europe or America. The North African style will be more informal and extremely hospitable, making the guest feel immediately like a member of the family. The European style will be more formal. Customs are changing all the time and one cannot be static in understanding them.

The meal to which a visitor might be invited will usually be lunch as the evening meal is often light, such as sandwiches. An invitation will probably be for about 12:30 p.m., as lunch may be at 1 p.m. A guest may bring a small gift for the house: flowers or candy. One should arrive on time in the European style, or arrive earlier, even at 9 in the morning in the more traditional style. Here, the host will say, "Come any time that you can", and he will mean it. In European style, the door will be opened by any member of the family; in traditional it would more often be by the host. One may spend about one-half hour in the living room and coffee and cold drinks will be served (wine and cocktails might be more often served in the evening with a special affair). The traditional household will serve a variety of things with the beverages such as nuts, cookies, and other snacks. Before entering the dining room one may wash hands, but this is not always done. The host sits at the head of the table, the hostess at the opposite end, usually near the kitchen. There may or may not be a Blessing before the meal, and if there is, it will be a blessing for the food or the wine. This may also be done on special days or for the new fruit or vegetable of the season. In European culture the oldest one starts eating first, in more traditional it would always be the host. Tablecloth, napkins and sometimes paper napkins are used. Conversation may be about all subjects and is flowing.

The meal consists of soup (sometimes), especially in cold weather, salad, meat, vegetables and dessert which may be strawberries, other fruits, ice cream, cake, or a fruit salad. Bread accompanies the meal and sometimes butter will be served.

In religious homes one eats only Kosher foods; no pork, no shell fish, and one cannot eat meat at the same time as cheese dishes or dishes made with milk. Vessels for cooking must be used only for certain foods. There will usually be an abundance of food available. Wine and beer or fruit juices or soda are offered and cold water, but not with ice in it. A guest may offer to help, which will be appreciated although the hostess will probably not permit it. When the meal is finished the host will stand up, then all rise and leave for the living room. In the more rural homes where the kitchen is a part of the general area, guests remain at the table, or move to a nearby chair. Coffee will be served and one should stay at least one hour to visit. If you are a very close friend you may be invited to spend the night, or your host may take you to show you the area and this will take some time. One must use his own judgment as to the time to leave, as each family is different and circumstances should dictate your timing.

When leaving, you may thank your hosts again, then later, before you leave the country you may send a card, flowers, a gift, or you may telephone to say goodbye. A letter from your homeland will be well received, especially if you tell about your travels, and you may invite them to visit you.

Gefulte Fisch (stuffed fish)

About 5 pounds of carp or pike or similar white fish
 using the entire fish
5 medium size onions (brown)
4 teaspoons salt and 2 teaspoons sugar
1 teaspoon sugar
2 beaten eggs (whole eggs)
1/2 cup cold water
1/4 cup matzo meal (can be bought at any store carrying Jewish foods)
2 sliced medium sized carrots
6 cups boiling water

Chop the fish and two of the onions fine. If you have a wooden bowl you should mix in that, otherwise use a regular mixing bowl. Put fish, onions, salt and pepper and sugar, matzo meal, eggs and cold

water in this bowl. Chop it all and mix until it is smoothly mixed.
Then put the fish head, skin and bones in a cooking pan and add
boiling water, some salt, pepper and carrots and boil it for one
instant. Roll the fish mix from the bowl into about two inch balls,
then put these into the liquid which is now boiling again. Cover it
and turn the heat low and cook for about one and one half hour; stir a
little now and then. Remove the balls gently. Strain the liquid and
put into a separate bowl. Serve very cold.

ITALY

Rome, an old historic city with modern
life, is the capital of this country
which has a Mediterranian climate. A
country of art and music, with a varied
history, its people forever seem to
adapt to the current state of life and
constantly enjoy being hosts to visitors
from every part of the world. The
religion is Roman Catholic although
other religions are practiced. The
Roman Empire has left its mark in every
area, but the more recent history dates
from 1870 with Italy's unification and,
after World War II, the government has
been characterized by political
turmoil.

Italians are a warm and expressive people who maintain a unique sense
of living. Through centuries of being under stresses of different
rules and having been used as a pathway during different wars, they
have learned to accept life as it comes, to rationalize and to make
the best of things.

Music has always been important to them and their enjoyment of beauty
is demonstrated by their architecture, their gardens, and many
artistic achievements which can be found in every city or village.

Italian dishes are a good example of this as they are not only tasty
but often artistic delights. A well set table can be a display of the
finest china, glassware and silver and flowers are used to give an
added glow to a festive meal.

Cooking is an ancient Italian art and, although it varies according to
region, one will always find the food enjoyable. Dishes are often
prepared to blend with a special (usually local) wine. The dinner
hour may be from about 8 to 10 o'clock--sometimes 7 p.m. in the
smaller towns, especially in the north when it becomes colder. One
should always arrive at the time invited. It is customary to bring a
small gift such as a box of chocolates or flowers, or if you know the
host well, any gift which you think is appropriate which may include a
bottle of wine or liquor. A servant or member of the family will
greet you at the door and escort you to the salon or living room for
an aperitif. This may be vermouth, brandy or whiskey, but usually not
a wine and never coffee. Sometimes this will be accompanied with hors
d'oeuvres. Visiting may continue here for one half to one hour, but
there is less drinking than in the United States and Italians do not
appreciate a guest who over indulges. All will go to the dining room
together where there will be a cloth and napkins on the table; place
mats are usually only used for breakfast. The host will sit at the

head of the table and the hostess at the opposite end, guests at the sides. There will be no butter plates, no butter, and the bread will be placed on the cloth near the main plate of each person. Often the host or others will say "buon appetito"; a guest may repeat this in response. Anti pasto soup and/or a pasta may be the first dish (pasta includes rice dishes, which the Italians prepare in my ways), meats (veal, fish, fowl, lamb and others), vegetables, and potatoes. Sometimes there will be salad (with vinegar and oil dressing) then dessert (cheese and fruits) and sometimes cakes or other dishes. The beverage will be wine and water cooled (but not ice). Coffee (Espresso) will be served after dinner in the living room and it will be strong and in small cups. This may be served with liquors or candies.

One may offer to help if there is no servant, but will probably not be permitted to do so. The dishes are often passed at the table or may be served to each person, but food is not served as a buffet from a side table. One can compliment the food but usually one does not request a recipe.

When leaving a thank you, "Grazie e'stata una bellissimi serata", which means thank you it has been a lovely evening, is a usual phrase. If you have not brought a gift when arriving, you may send flowers afterwards, but this is not expected, and notes are not sent. Do not send crysanthemums as these are usually used for funerals. A letter from your homeland will be welcome. There is a delicious dish from northern Italy which is also a conversation piece. Once upon a time a hunter went to the country to get some birds for dinner for his family. Unfortunately for him, there were no birds that day and he had to come home empty handed. His wife, who loved him very much and did not want him to be unhappy, disappeared into the kitchen. When dinner time arrived she served a great dish of polenta with little fake birds all around the edge. Of course this had to be called "Uccelli Scappati", or the birds which escaped. To this day this dish is popular, especially in families where there are hunters.

POLENTA SERVED ON A WOODEN BOARD

Uccelli Scappati

Cut veal cutlets (pounded) into thin slices, cut kidneys same, about the size of a quarter, cut bacon same, alternate slices on a thick stick or skewer. Salt and pepper and add a few other spices if desired (you may add a slice of mushroom). All should be kept small to resemble the size of a wild bird. Fry these and save all the juices. Put them around a basin of polenta and fill the basin with the juices.

Polenta

In English this is called corn meal, although it is usually not ground as polenta and therefore does not make the same dish. One should go to an Italian store to buy the true polenta.

To one cup of polenta use 4 cups of water and 1 1/2 tablespoons salt.

Bring salted water to a boil, stir into it the polenta, slowly, stir with a long handled wooden spoon until the polenta leaves the side of the pan. It should be stiffer than porridge. This may take about 20 minutes or more. Put polenta on a dish and form it into a bowl shape.

Ossobuco alla Milanese

(translated, osso means bone and buco means hole)
This is a Milanese specialty which is enjoyed throughout Italy.

First melt 50 grams of butter in a pan with one chopped onion and cook until butter is slightly brown; and 4 ossi buchi (these beef bones are from the leg and are round with marrow filling in the center hole). Ossi buchi are cut in small pieces about 1 1/2 inches thick. Dip these in flour, being sure all the meat and bone is well covered with the flour. Now add one glass of white wine, and when this has been absorbed, add one glass of hot meat broth or boullion a little at a time. Cook over a low fire for about one hour in a covered pan. The sauce should become about as thick as cream. Ten minutes before serving, add a bit of chopped prezzemolo. (Prezzemolo is Italian parsley with a broader leaf than most American parsley and a different flavor). Serve with plain boiled rice using the sauce on the rice.

JAPAN

The bustling city of Tokyo is Japan's capital which is a mixture of old and seems to be filled with an abundance of moving vehicles. Japan's climate ranges from subtropical to cool. The summers are rainy and the winters are sunny. Because of the population and rainfall the cultivation of the land is dense. Japanese is the official language and religions include Buddhism, Shintoism, Christianity and Confucianism. The country is a mixture of tradition and modern and one can see both at the same time in almost any area. Originally an Empire, the rulers were respected as descendants of the Sun Goddess and therefore were sacred. Later, after the Second World War, the government developed into a parliamentary rule with the Emperor known as the symbol of the state. Customs are sometimes difficult for a foreigner to interpret.

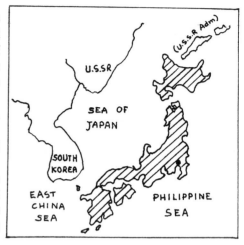

In order to get a more real feeling of the Japanese life, a visitor should spend some time in Japanese inns. Here you will find a pleasant room with practically no furniture. There will be a small dressing table in front of which you must sit on the floor to use the mirror and there may be one or two other low tables. The floor will be spotless and covered with the usual Tatami, or woven straw mat. Your shoes must be removed before entering the room and a kimono, the Japanese native costume, a robe-like garment will be provided for each guest along with a feather comforter which will be rolled out on the floor for sleeping. There are no western style beds. A bathroom is attached and has in it the customary washing materials: a small wooden stool, soap, a towel, sometimes a scrubbing brush, a small wooden bucket for rinsing and the tub. It is customary to wash your body thoroughly and rinse with the bucket. Japanese never wash in the tub, but soak in hot water in it after rinsing. The water is kept hot sometimes by a fire which is in a section of the tub and is usually about 120° F. The tub is wooden and only large enough for a person to remain in a sitting position with the knees drawn up near the chin. The same hot soaking water is used by all who bathe at this time. You will not find large or communal baths in most inns as these are usually in specific hotels or inns having access to special water or hot springs. Public baths are also large and many soak at the same time. Breakfast will be served in your room where it is placed on a low table. You will eat sitting on the floor Japanese style. There may be soup, sea weed, always rice, always tea and sometimes other seafood items. If you are a true adventurer you will find these breakfasts delightful, light yet satisfying.

A Japanese cooking vessel called the Hibachi is used like a barbecue in which foods may be cooked over a fire. Legend has it that this vessel evolved from the campaigns of Genghis Kahn. All the equipment for his armies including cooking utensils, had to be carried on horseback, but the vessels were metal and very heavy. So Genghis Kahn took off his helmet, turned it upside down put some food in it and cooked over the fire. Now, the soldiers could wear their helmets by day and cook in them at meal times. To this day, the Hibachi has the shape of a warring helmet.

When invited for dinner, guests may arrive five to ten minutes late as it is polite to allow the hosts to be fully ready. Instead of being invited to a home, guests are often asked to go to a restaurant. The dinner may be from 5 to 8 to 9 p.m. Before dinner Sake the national beverage (a rice wine) is served. This is done in very small ceramic cups and is drunk hot. It is polite to fill each other's cups; the host fills the guest's and then the guest fills the host's. Each time the cup must be filled to the very top, each holding his own while the other pours, and each time each person says thank you. One can safely consume only two or three of these cups full, always holding the cup in the right hand partly supported with the left.

The Tokonoma is the most honored place to sit in the home. This will include a scroll on the wall and a flower arrangement on a low table beneath it. The idea is to form a most flattering background for the person who sits in front of it. The Tokonoma has nothing to do with religion. Since it is a very special place, the visitor, if he is of high esteem such as a president or great celebrity, will be told to sit there, although this custom is not as strict as in the past. A guest will always refuse this place, insisting that the host sit there, but eventually should give in.

When eating, people sit on the floor on a Tatami. A low table is in the center and one sits on his knees. The Tokonoma will be at one end and the place near at the side will be for the guest. Guests sit on one side and hosts on the other facing them; no one will be at the far end. Before eating one says, "itadakimasu", meaning, "I am going to eat now".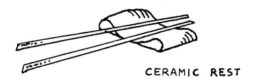

CERAMIC REST

Chopsticks are used but if you cannot handle them you may ask for a fork. If there is a main dish from which the food is served, you may use a set of sticks put there for that purpose, or the opposite ends of your own are sometimes used for serving yourself. Usually the foods will be in separate small bowls. A guest is often

TOKANOMA

invited to begin by taking some from a main dish. When your sticks are not in use they may be placed on a ceramic holder near your bowl, or if they are wrapped in paper and there is no holder take wrapping paper off and rest them on it. Often this will be tied in a knot and placed by your plate.

Rice is eaten all the time and miso soup is almost as popular. Rice is not flavored and is cooked to a sticky consistancy, easy to pick up with sticks. Soup is drunk from the bowl, holding it with one or both hands, there are no spoons. When eating, drink some, then eat some, try to finish everything at the same time. Tea, very hot, is served with the meal. It is permissible to make a noise while drinking, by pulling air through the front teeth. Japanese pickles are almost a must at each meal. These are to freshen the mouth and are good at the end of the meal. They are called o-tsukemono oro-shinko. Soya sauce may be used for many dishes and hot mustard with raw fish, "sashimi". Napkins are not used. While in a formal meal one never picks up the bowl, in a casual setting the bowl is held in one hand and chop sticks in the other. Usually rice will be put in the bottom and other items on top with the sauce. The appearance of the food is very important in Japan. Green tea is the national beverage but coffee is popular and whiskey or other hard liquors are widely used. The dessert, which may be cakes, will be served with tea.

After dinner, before the dessert, one may say thank you for the meal. Thank you is "gochisosama". All will linger at the table unless they are requested to move to another area. When you think you wish to leave, get up and leave quickly, saying thank you and goodnight. There is no handshaking, just deep bows to each other, although strangers need not bow if it is awkward for them.

A letter of thanks may be sent but no flowers. A gift may be sent if it is not too large. When you have brought a gift upon arriving, do not send one later. It is always polite to call or telephone to say goodbye when you leave the country, and to write a letter from your home.

JORDAN

Amman is the capital of Jordan, an arid country of deserts, mountains and plains. Most of the population is near the Jordan River as there is not enough rainfall elsewhere to sustain vegetation. It has a Mediterranian climate. Most Jordanians come from Arab stock and the official language is Arabic, although English is widely spoken. Originally Jordan was a part of the Ottoman empire and later was under British domination until 1946 when it became the Hashemite Kingdom of Jordan. The religion is Sunni Muslim and some Christianity.

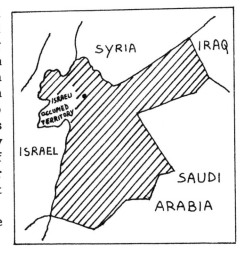

One is usually invited to lunch instead of dinner as this is the main meal. Lunch is from about 12 noon to 2 p.m. but you may arrive at any time. Often a host will say, "I invite you for lunch" (time not given). You may arrive any time from 9 a.m. to 12 noon, or even 2 o'clock. The average eating time will be about 1 o'clock. You may bring a gift, especially if for the children, or food, but no wine unless it is a Christian family because the Muslims will not drink anything with alcohol in it. If you are a male guest, the host will greet you at the door and if you are a female, the hostess will greet you. A wife may be home all day so that you may arrive early but if a husband works he may come home shortly before the meal time. Thus, if you are a male you should time your arrival for when he will be there.
 If guests are close friends they will go to the family room. If not, they will sit in the parlor until the meal is ready. The furniture will be of European style. Coca cola, soft drinks, lemon juice, or orange juice is served while people visit. If it is a Christian family there may be hard liquor. Before anything else Jordanians always drink Arabic coffee. Men have three cups and women have two. If you wish no more coffee you simply shake your cup. Hands are washed before and after every meal. Before eating Christians often say Grace, and all say, "Daimeh Alhamdelah", meaning thanks to God.

There will be meat (Muslims will not eat pork) and rice with nuts and other condiments on a large platter. The meat will be cooked to tenderness and one uses the fingers to break pieces off, always using the right hand only. A fork and spoon may be used for the rice. Cut the meat with the right hand, eat with the fork in the left, eating a spoonful of rice after each bite of meat. If you eat with a knife, fork and spoon, put the fork on the edge of the plate when using the spoon. All food should be eaten, none should be left on your plate. The hostess will offer you the choice pieces and you may also help yourself. Usually there will be lamb and probably no vegetables with

Mansaff, which is the rice-meat dish. Other meals may have vegetables, rice, potatoes, and tomatoes. The vegetables are often fried in oil.

Some say it is polite to say the food is good and especially if it is from the host's garden. Others think it is better not to discuss food.

After washing hands, all will return to the previous room where visiting continues while fruit such as apples, oranges and grapes, backlava or other sweets are served on a large plate. Individual plates are offered with a knife and a napkin. The fruit is eaten with fingers and is a refreshing end to a sometimes heavy but delicious meal.

Jordanians will not expect a thank you note or gift, but it will be appreciated if you write a letter from your country and remind them of the pleasure which they gave you, and invite them to visit if you wish.

KENYA

The center of Nairobi, the capitol of Kenya, is within a few miles distance of a native African game reserve, where one driving through sees various species in their native habitat contrasted with the modern buildings of this large city. Kenya is on the equator and has arid and dry sections and some tropical areas on the coast. Its Great Rift Valley is vast and dramatic and its mountain, Mt. Kenya, rises majestically from the valley. The ethnic make-up of the population is Kikuyu, Luo, Baluhyu, Kamba, Kisii and Meru. Most of the people are farmers. Although there are some Protestants, Catholics and Muslims, many follow their traditional religions or have no religion. English is the official language but almost all speak Swahili and many other African tongues. Influence and rule over the country has been by Africans, Arabs, Portuguese and British. Self government began in 1964.

In modern Kenya, dinner can be any time between seven and nine o'clock, usually not at a fixed time. One may bring a gift to a host or hostess especially if there are children in the family, but this is not expected. Usually the host and hostess will greet you at the door and escort you to the living room where you will be offered soft drinks or cocktails, whiskey, wine, or coffee or tea. There are usually no hors d'oeuvres, but there may be cookies. Here you may spend about fifteen minutes and will probably have one drink only. On the way to the dining room you may wash your hands in the rest room. The dining table may be round, square or oblong with a white cloth, although sometimes there will be place mats and paper napkins. The silverware will be of the usual western style. The host and hostess sit at opposite ends and guests at the sides. Some families say Grace and some do not. One eats when served and usually the food is passed by the diners, or a platter may be placed in the center of the table. Often there will be a maid to help. Dinner may consist of soup, bread (seldom butter), meat, potatoes or rice or corn, boiled vegetables, no salad, fruits such as pineapple, bananas, pau pa or oranges, or a mixed salad of fruits. Grilled meat is popular, such as steak, beef or goat. Salt and pepper the meat, and grill. Not much seasoning is used in the cooking and any part of the animal may be used, in any shape. Usually there will just be water to drink with the meal. There are seldom cakes. A cup of coffee may be offered to you either here or when you return to the living room. You will stay there for at least one half to one hour and more drinks may be served while you talk or watch television. You may compliment the food, but usually it is best not to offer to help.

The people of Kenya are hospitable and will take great pleasure in telling you about their country and their people.

In a more traditional style, your invitation might be "for the evening" and you should arrive between six and seven o'clock. You will not be offered anything to drink as your host and hostess will lead you directly to the room where you will eat. You may sit on the floor or sometimes there may be a table. Before eating you will exchange greetings, then wash your hands. You may either eat with utensils or with your fingers, especially if the food is ribs or chicken legs. The food will be the same as in the more modern meal, except that it will be cooked together as a stew. If the food is served on a table you may still eat from your lap. The hostess serves each person and there will be no napkins. Beverages may be water, coffee, tea or milk. Hands are always washed again after eating.

When leaving you may thank your hosts at the door. Notes are not customarily written but you may invite your host to your hotel for a meal if you wish. A small gift may be sent but this is also not customarily done. When leaving the country you should call to say goodbye. A letter from your homeland will be appreciated.

KUWAIT

The easiest name of the capital of a country to remember is Kuwait, for it is the same name as the country. Kuwaitis are Arab by origin but only about one half of them are indigenous as many have come and continue to come from sur rounding countries, including many Iranians. The original population is Sunni Muslim, as to religion, and Arabic is the official language, although English is understood widely. Kuwait has been under Turkish rule, has been connected to Britian by treaty influence and in 1961 became independent with a constitutional monarchy. The women live  separately from the men and mothers, sisters and female friends and relatives will be together in a home. Even if there is a husband and wife the men will go with their group and the women will join the other females. Sometimes when there is a foreign visitor, they may sit together in the salon or living room but even then they will dine separately.

Usually an invitation will be for lunch rather than dinner. One may arrive at 11:45 or 12 o'clock and the actual meal will probably be at one o'clock. You may bring a gift if it comes from another country, or flowers, but never any alcoholic beverage. If you are a man you will be greeted by a man at the man's door and if you are a woman you will be met by a woman at the woman's door. There are two living rooms, one for each sex. Even if you arrive as a couple, you will probably go to the separate rooms. You may shake hands but most close friends embrace each other when greeting. The living room may have European style furniture or Arab style tables with rugs and covered pads for sitting. Tea, Arabian coffee, Coca-Cola and other soft drinks will be served and you may stay here and visit for about one hour. Wines and liquors are not used in Muslim homes.

Hands are usually washed in bowls near the room. When there are no chairs all sit on the floor on a rug around a central floor covering on which the food is placed. Sometimes chairs will be specially

provided for foreign guests. There may be seven or eight large serving dishes and there will not be any napkins. The foods will be rice with meat on it, many spices, sometimes very hot, and all are eaten with fingers using the right hand only. There may be a whole lamb. When there is soup it is served in individual bowls. Pork is never eaten in Muslim families. Salad will probably have vinegar and oil dressing and vegetables may include potatoes and beans. All this may be followed by fruits such as cantaloupe, oranges, apples, or watermelon and the fruit is usually placed behind the guests and then served by a servant or the host. Other desserts may be custards, puddings, cake. The bread is large, round and flat and one can use it to scoop up the food. Milk or water will be served. If there are servants, the men servants serve the men and the women servants serve the women. There is usually a large variety of foods from which to choose. Your host will be pleased if you enjoy the dishes, but you should not take more of each than you can eat. Conversation is expected during the meal. At the beginning of the meal a saying will be, "In the name of merciful God we start our food". After the meal one should say that the food is good. Then hands are again washed and usually a cologne is offered to freshen the skin.

The visiting time when all returned to another room is from about one half hour to one hour depending upon the circumstances. "Shukran" is the word for thank you and one does not send a gift or a note nor does he telephone to thank the hosts. He should, however, telephone to say goodbye when leaving the country and then write from home to invite his friends to visit.

LAOS

Laos is very strategically located in the peninsula of southeast Asia. It is a kingdom and has two capitals; Vientiane which is the administrative one and a royal one called Loung-phrabang. There are monsoons and heavy rainfall. The humidity is high and the heat can be intense. About half the people are descendants of Tais while other ethnic groups who came in early times are found in some areas. It is a mixed population and has no common origin, language, religion. The main religion is Theravada Buddhism but sometimes this is mixed with other beliefs. The main language is Lao but French is spoken as an official and second language.

The dinner hour is at about six in the evening and you should arrive at the time you are invited, never late. Neither gifts nor flowers are brought to your hosts. There are modern and traditional customs and if you are in a city you may eat in European style. You will be greeted at the door and escorted to a living room or directly to a dining room where there will be western style furniture. Sometimes you may wash your hands and sometimes not, depending upon the family. Seating arrangements are usually very informal. In a village one eats in an outside room with a wooden floor.

There will be a small round very low bamboo table. People sit on the floor and eat with their hands and a metal spoon. Cloth napkins are used. For these meals hands are always washed in a bowl outside. You may sit anywhere and there is no special saying or Grace before the meal. The guest begins and the host will show him how to eat if he hesitates or shows that he

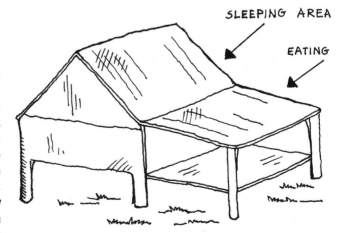

SLEEPING AREA

EATING

does not know what to do. Everything is on the table and you should take what you want but be sure to taste everything as this is an old and important custom. All eat from the same plates. Sometimes there will be water to drink or sometimes plant-root water or juice. The meal may consist of chicken, beef or pork or all of these, cut into small pieces. There will be a large variety of vegetables, except carrots and potatoes, and the rice will be cooked to a sticky consistency. Bread is not used. There may be fruits or a fruit soup which is sweet and this is called "Nam wan", which translates to "sweet water".

There is no conversation as the thought is that this is the time for eating and the visiting hour will come later. At the end of the meal a gesture of praying hands, without any speaking, signifies that the dinner is finished.

Before the visiting time hands are again washed and the visit should last as long as possible. Do not leave early if you can avoid it. You should compliment the food before leaving. In the city where customs are more European, one should stay after the meal from about one half to two hours and not too long if the host must rise early the next morning.

Thank you, "Kobchai", translates literally to, Kob-circle and chai-heart. In this there is a gentle friendliness expressed which illustrates something about the character of these people.

BAMBOO TABLE

LEBANON

Beirut, the capital of Lebanon, has been drastically damaged by fighting in recent years and this has changed its appearance from a city with great modern buildings to one of sad signs of destruction. Surely the city will one day regain its architectural enhancement as its location is climatically and practically desirable and the people will never leave this area. The climate is truly Mediterranean. The Lebanese are divided into almost half Christian and half Muslim and the Christians include Maronites, Greek Orthodox and Armenians. The official language is

Arabic, but Armenian, French and English are widely spoken. This is the historical land and home of the Phoenicians and Roman ruins are plentiful. The French have had great influence in Lebanon and an American University is located in a park-like setting by the sea.

It is difficult to describe a Lebanese as the nation contains an astonishing mixture of races. Its location, not only on the sea, but also on the Syrian highway, links Lebanon to Europe, Asia and Africa. Because the country has had numerous invasions, there is little ethnic unity. The original Phoenician strain which was that of the people who inhabited the area around the Mediterranean was probably the major source from which the Lebanese came. However, this has been added to and constantly changing because of those persons who came with the conquests, the travellers, people in trade, or those who settled here for a variety of other reasons. The result is that the Lebanese are extremely interested in the affairs of the world and are known world-wide for their business ability and their proficiency as bankers. They are energetic and efficient in architectural achievements also. Mosques, cathedrals and modern buildings attest to this. Night life, usually in night clubs, as in many Middle Eastern countries is enthusiastically enjoyed. The people are colorful, interesting, and very pleasant to visit.

Lebanese time depends upon who invites the guest, or whether you are a male or female (a male will be at work, a female will be at home). Lunch is from one to two o'clock and the evening meal is from six to seven. You must arrive after working hours unless you know the hostess and yet you will probably have been invited for "whenever you want". A man will never arrive at a home before the husband has come home unless he knows the wife very well and even then, he usually waits until the man of the house is sure to be present. If you persuade your hosts to give you a specific time he will probably say dinner will be at nine. You must arrive then at 8:30 or 8 p.m., but you may come any time before that. The Lebanese custom is to arrive

at any time during the day. You could even arrive as early as nine or
ten in the morning. You will always be offered tobacco and coffee in
the living room. Of course, if it is a family who lives by the French
customs they will expect you to arrive at the hour for which you were
invited, and their manners of eating and entertaining you will be
almost the same as in Europe. A gift or flowers may be brought to
your hosts. The hostess will usually greet and escort you to the
salon or living room where you may find either European or American
modern influence in the furniture. There will be a relaxed time for
talking. In warm weather you may be offered lemonade, fruit juices or
Coca-Cola and in cold weather, tea, strong coffee and liquors such as
brandy and cognac.

The dining table is usually only an archway away from the salon and
the two rooms may blend. The table will be set with the usual cloth,
napkins (not paper), and silverware. Hands are washed in a separate
room before eating and again when the meal is completed. Sometimes
the drinking water will be served in a pitcher to be poured directly
into the mouth as one does with wine from a wine skin. If you cannot
accomplish this feat (and it does take skill), you should ask for an
individual glass. Arak is a popular drink and ice (which changes the
flavor) may be added only as you drink it. Do not be fooled by its
innocently clean, fresh taste. It is very strong and to be
unaccustomed, it may have a quick and resounding effect.

All the dishes will be on the table and there may be over 40. Using a
metal spoon or using Pita bread to serve, you may eat directly from
the main dishes. The cold dishes are consumed first, using something
like the idea of an Italian antipasto of vegetables both cooked or
raw, raw meat ground or in chunks, and raw liver. Hot dishes will be
meats in small pieces prepared in five or six ways, chicken, fish,
etc. All these are called "Meza". There will be salads and cheese.
"Labne" is something between cheese and yogurt. Also there is much
pure French cooking in Lebanon. Pork is usually not eaten in the
Muslim families although some do now eat it. You must learn to reach
far if you are to enjoy your meal and you will be expected to take up
to two hours or more for dinner. You may smoke a pipe, the
hubble-bubble or argeelee, and use the same coals for the pipe which
were used for barbecuing most of the meats. Fruit is offered after
all the plates have been removed and often there are cakes or ices.
You may always use your knife and fork if you wish, especially to cut
the meat. If you wish beer it is polite to request it in the place of
arak or whiskey, or you may decline any alcoholic beverage and ask for
water or Coca-Cola. As in most European countries, excessive
drinking is considered to be very bad manners. Do say the food is
good and don't hesitate to talk during the meal. When you finish
eating, if using utensils, the fork and knife should be placed on your
plate in a crossed position and the napkin placed beside the plate.
Coffee may be served at the table or in the salon, which is more
customary. If you smoke, do not smoke your own cigarettes but always
those which are offered you. There will usually be many varieties at

your disposal, often on a small bar which will have cognac and whiskey. Sometimes chocolates are served after dinner. Visiting and discussion, especially politics, will be from one half to one hour but you may stay later depending upon the circumstances. The Lebanese will, as many people in this part of the world, insist that you eat more and stay longer. It is polite to decline and to be firm.

"Merci" is a recognized word for thank you in Lebanon and if you have not brought a gift or flowers you may send one later with a note if you wish, although this is not necessary. You may call when leaving to say goodbye, or you may write from home and invite them to visit if you desire, but this also is not necessary.

MALAYSIA

Kuala Lumpur, a city which is intensively interesting to visitors partly because of its ruins, is the capital of Malaysia. The population is a mixture of Malays, Indians, Chinese and others. Their religions are Muslim, Hindu, Buddhist and Christian. The languages are Malay, Chinese (in varying dialects) English and Tamil. Malaysia is made up of two areas which are separated by four hundred miles of the South China Sea. These are often referred to as West and East Malaysia.

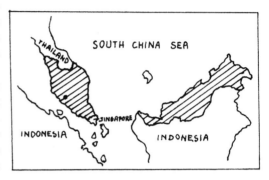

Two states in the eastern part of Malaysia are called Sarawak and Sabah and in between these is the oil rich country of Brunei. War between Malaysia and Indonesia was fought over this small piece of land. The most dense population is in the western part of West Malaysia which consists of eleven states. Early history goes back to Portuguese rule in 1511, then Dutch and later English. This lasted until World War II when the Japanese occupied the country. There was bitter fighting and the natives suffered greatly during this time; cruel punishments are still spoken of today. There are monsoons and much swampland and tropical jungle.

Because of this equatorial climate, tropical fruits abound, one of which is Durian. This is believed to be the most nutritious fruit in the world. However, it must ripen on the tree and is not considered ready to eat until it has fallen to the ground. When this occurs the odor is very strong and you can smell it from a very long distance. A neighbor will always know when someone else's fruit is ripe just by this odor which has been compared to "rotten socks", or onions. Nevertheless, whatever a visitor might think, this is a pleasant smell to Malayians and the fruit is treasured. The fruit is green to yellowish and the meat is a whitish yellow. Some may have a slightly fermented taste but generally it is sweet and has a texture not unlike that of an avocado.

Dinner may be from 7:30 or 8 o'clock. One may arrive a little early, one hour early or up to twenty minutes late. You may bring a gift or flowers or food, but no alcoholic beverages. The host and hostess will greet you at the door and always shake your hand. Then, they will escort you to the living room where the furniture will be of western style and you will be offered tea, coffee and soft drinks with Malay cakes. Here you will visit for about one hour unless you have arrived on time for the meal, which means that all will go directly to the table; the visit may be short or not at all. The dining table may be any shape and may have a cloth and often paper napkins and some silverware.

Muslims say a prayer before eating but with a foreign guest this is often not done. The meal may consist of rice with fish or chicken or meat, no pork and no potatoes unless they are with curry and very hotly spiced. The beverage will be water. Salad is eaten with the meal and usually with a pre-mixed dressing of vinegar and oil. Dessert may be fruit cocktail or cakes. Strong coffee accompanies the meal. There is usually a servant and one does not offer to help. Conversation continues throughout the meal and you should compliment the food. In the living room the conversation continues but no more refreshments are served. One should stay for at least one half hour and leave as the conversation begins to seem finishing.

"Terima kaseh" is the word for thank you. You may send a note, telephone, send flowers or invite your hosts to your hotel, but the important thing that you must do is call them when you are leaving the country to say goodbye. A letter from your homeland will be appreciated.

Nasi (Rice)

This is the simple basic recipe used by many Asian countries to cook rice. However, Nasi Lemak contains coconut milk and is often used with the fish or chicken recipes. For this, use 4 1/2 cups of coconut milk in place of the water. The rice is scooped on the plate and the fish or chicken sauces are put on top of it. Often these are eaten with fresh cucumbers.

2 cups rice
4 1/2 cups water

Add the two and boil over stove at medium heat. Cover lid. When boiled, lower heat until it is cooked.

Curry Daging (Meat) or Ayam (Chicken)

1 tablespoon curry powder
2 tablespoons cooking oil (olive)

1 pound meat or chicken
Onions, potatoes, Carnation milk, salt and chicken cubes

Heat oil in a pot. Fry onions until brown. Put in curry powder which has been mixed with 3 tablespoons water. Lower heat until powder is cooked. Add in the meat or chicken, potatoes and salt. Add some water if it is rather dry. When meat or chicken have become tender, add in the milk--amount depending on how much gravy you want. Note: For fish curry--same method is being followed except that you add the fish after you've put in the milk. At the same time, add some 'ayer asam jawa' (tamarind water) if you have any, otherwise squeeze some lemon.

Ikan Bakar (Grilled fish)

1 fish	4 chillis
1 onion	Milk, salt, lemon juice

Clean fish and sprinkle some salt. Leave it under the grill for some time, turning once. Cut onions and chillis in small pieces. Mix some salt into onions and chillis and squeeze some lemon juice into them. Add in some milk and 2 tablespoons water. Pour mixture over the fish and leave under the grill to cook.

Masak Lemak Sayor (Vegetable)

1/4 cabbage
1 onion
Chillis, (udang kering) dried shrimp, milk

Boil cabbage with onions, chillis and dried shrimp. Do not put in too much water. Add some salt. When cabbage is soft, add some milk for gravy and let it boil.

Kerabu

1 cucumber	1 onion
1 tomato	2 tablespoons vinegar, a pinch of salt and sugar

Cut cucumber, tomato and onion in small pieces. Mix all together.

MEXICO

Mexico City, the capital of Mexico, is a city of much activity with a blend of old and modern buildings. Nearby, at Chapultapec Park there is a museum which explains the past; the Indians who lived in this part of the world had a very high civilization established by the Olmecs, Mayas, Toltecs and Aztecs. Their pyramids dominate some of the cities and a visitor finds endless points of interest while wandering among the ruins. After years of domination by Spain a Republic was established in 1822. The people of Mexico are a mixture of Spanish and Indian with the  Indian predominating, or "Mestizos". Their religion is Roman Catholic and their climate varies but most of it is dry. Flowers abound where there is sufficient rainfall. Mexicans are colorful and hospitable and enjoy showing visitors their land and their culture.

"Chicanos" are those persons who have been born in the United States from Mexican parents and who usually prefer to be known as Mexicans or Mexican-Americans. Many have had difficult times adjusting to life in the States and often have been discriminated against. Obviously many feel that they are second-class citizens and often have grouped together, not entering into the mainstream of American life. Some Americans judge all Mexicans by the few whom they see around them even though they may never know them well enough to be on speaking terms. Mexicans are variable and differ from area to area even within their own country. See the map marking the various Mexican States, the end of this section.

Often tourists become upset physically while travelling in Mexico and blame it on the food or water but few realize that this sort of sickness generally can be avoided by using a few precautions. When arriving by airplane in Mexico City a visitor should immediately rest for about one hour in order to acclimate to the change of altitude. Foods can be quite different from those in most other countries and should be taken in small quantities until you are accustomed to them. Water is potable in many parts of Mexico, but if you have trouble adjusting to it the simplest way to avoid being upset is to buy bottled water or drink beer or wine or fruit juices which are natural. An interesting note is that many Mexicans are disturbed by the foods or water in other countries when they travel. Your personal physician can probably supply you with medicine to take with you as an extra precaution if you are especially susceptible to this kind of illness. But, in any event, do not let it deter you from visiting this enjoyable and interesting country.

Mexican food always tastes better when guests are surrounded with the music of the Marriachis. These musicians are ever present in Mexico and are a part of the every-day culture. They are always male and they wear a costume which resembles an elegant black or very dark suit with silver embroidered decorations; their hats are also decorated with the same silver patterns. Their music is loud and a little like marching music. Instruments include a guitar, a violin and trumpets. Sometimes a harp will also be used, but not often. The music is native and lively. There are, as in other countries strolling violinists who may sing native love songs, but the Marriachis are the most typical to Mexico. Seranading is still popular in this country.

Dinner may be at about 8:30 or 9 in the evening. You should arrive on time but not early and you may bring wine, flowers or cookies or cake or other dessert which will be shared by all. Anyone in the family may greet you and escort you to the salon or living room where you will visit for from one half to one hour. All kinds of beverages may be served accompanied by peanuts, dip and potato chips or other snacks. Mexico produces very good beer and is also known for its Tequila which is used in its special Margarita cocktails. These will always have a coating of salt around the rim of the glass in which they are served and they are a very popular drink. After the cocktail hour you will enter the dining room were a cloth and napkins are usually on the table with the standard silverware. Couples usually are seated together. Grace is said only now and then. The hostess will begin to eat first. You may offer to help if you wish. There may be wine and sometimes water, but very often beer will be served with a Mexican meal. The dinner may consist of soup, salad, meat, fish or fowl, vegetables and dessert. Some foods, such as turkey, may have a mole (made with Mexican chocolate) sauce which at times may be so hot that it will bring tears to your eyes. There is a shrimp stew which may do the same, but often the food is not very hotly spiced. Eggs are eaten in many ways and tortillas may take the place of bread at some meals. These may be placed flat in your hand, or on your plate, filled with re-fried beans or other ingredients rolled into a cigar shape and folded over on one end to keep the filling from falling out. One eats them from the open end holding them with the fingers. Tortillas may also be eaten with butter and they are always served hot. After the meal, all will return to the living room where coffee and liquor, such as the well known Kahlua, will be served. One may remain after dinner from about one hour to any time depending upon what the family may plan. Often card games will go into the early morning hours.

"Gracias, la cena estuba deliciosa" means thank you, the dinner was delicious. Thank you notes are not sent but you may telephone and thank your hosts again. A letter from your home after you have returned to your country will be welcome.

Tortillo

In order to make true tortillas you should use a flour which is called masa. This is made of corn which is boiled, dried and ground and then refined with a metate. Masa is mixed with water only, no salt. Make a small ball of the flour and water in your hands. Cut a circle from paper, such as a plastic bag. Now, using the palm of your hand, pat and constantly turn the ball until it flattens patting it constantly with the paper in your hand. When it is about 5 inches in circumference it will be the right size. (Some people do not use the paper but just pat with their hands). Heat a heavy fry pan to very hot but do not put any oil or grease into it. Then put the tortilla in it and cook for one minute on each side, do not over cook. Good masa will not stick to the pan. Serve very hot. To keep hot you may put them in a covered dish or cover them with a linen cloth.

States and Territories

1. Baja California
2. Territorio de Baja California
3. Sonora
4. Chihuahua
5. Coahuila
6. Nuevo León
7. Tamaulipas
8. Sinaloa
9. Durango
10. Zacatecas
11. San Luis Potosi
12. Nayarit
13. Aguascalientes
14. Veracruz
15. Jalisco
16. Guanajuato
17. Querétaro
18. Hidalgo
19. Colima
20. Michoacán
21. México
22. Puebla
24. Tlaxcala
25. Guerrero
26. Morelos
27. Oaxaca
28. Tabasco
29. Chiapas
30. Campeche
31. Yucatán
32. Territorio de Quintana Roo

23. DISTRITO FEDERAL

MOROCCO

Rabat is the capital of Morocco and it is a coast city on the Atlantic Ocean. The chief ethnic groups in the country are Arabs, Berbers, Negroes and French. Arab is the official language and French and Berber dialects are spoken also. Everyone recognizes that Western civilization owes much to the ancient Greeks, but few know that the information did not always reach Europe directly from Greece. The Moors were extremely interested in mathematics and they re-discovered much of the Greek legacy. Between the ninth and the twelfth centuries they were the interpreters of this legacy in Spain. There were many Moroccan scholars especially in the city of Fez and an exchange of scholars existed between Fez and the city of Cordova in Spain. Other influences came through Sicily where the Moors mixed with Sicilians and natives of other countries.

Morocco has high mountains, some of which rise sharply from the coast and some plains, plateaus and desert. The climate varies but is sunny and pleasant on the coastal side of the Mediterranean. The population is very unevenly distributed because of the topography and the climate. Since the time of the Phoenician there have been many invasions and Morocco has been ruled by the Romans, the Vandals, the Visigoths, and Byzantine Greeks. Later, Islamic Arabs occupied the country and there was also a period of French and Spanish dominance. The religion is Islamic. Morocco is now a Kingdom and has been independent since 1956.

The dinner hour is at about 7 p.m. or later, but a more formal invitation would be for lunch. One should arrive from 20 to 30 minutes early. If you are invited for lunch you may bring a small gift, but it is not customary to do so for a dinner. In a modern home the person who invited you will probably greet and escort you to the salon or living room where mint tea and wine may be served. After a short visit all will wash their hands in another room and then proceed to the dining room, usually led by the host. There will be a round table with a cloth, cloth napkins and the usual silverware. Usually a prayer or Grace are not said before the meal. The host and hostess will serve and the meal may consist of a salad with oil and vinegar dressing, sometimes soup, meat, fish or fowl, (but no pork) potatoes, kuskus (a grain prepared like steamed rice), vegetables, fruit, milk, wine or water without ice. Conversation is plentiful and covers many subjects. One does not offer to help.

The host will lead all back to the salon where there may be coffee,

mint tea, and sometimes liquor. It is customary to remain from about
one half hour to one and one half an hour after the meal. You may
thank you hosts and then, if you wish, you may send a small gift to
the house, or flowers, but not a thank you note. When you arrive in
your own country you may write them a letter with an invitation to
visit you.

In a traditional home there will almost always be a servant who greets
the guest and during the visiting time of about one half hour there
will be mint tea only; no wine or liquor as the hosts will adhere
strictly to their religious rules. You will be served Moroccan
pastries with your teas. Water is brought to wash hands and there
will be soap and towel. There will be no separate dining room and you
will eat in a part of the living room. The table will be low with a
cloth on it and in the place of chairs there will be ottomans. Here
you will eat with your fingers using the right hand only. The host
will give a blessing and then begin to eat. He will serve with a
spoon from the center dish. There will be a spoon for the soup and
the food may be the same as in the modern setting, but there will not
be any wine. Conversation will flow all through the meal and a prayer
of thanks is said at the end. Water will be brought again to wash and
coffee and mint tea will be served.

The same general rules apply to the time you should remain and how you
should thank your hosts as with the modern family. "Shokrun" is the
word for thank you and it is very polite to praise the food.

Morocca (lamb)

1 cup white raisins
Dry sherry
1/2 cup vegetable oil
3 pounds lean lamb shoulder, cut
   into 1 1/2 cubes
1 large onion, finely chopped
Salt and freshly ground pepper to taste
Red pepper flakes to taste

1 teaspoon ground tumeric
3 large tomatoes, peeled and
   chopped
1 cup (approximately) chicken stock
   stock
1 cup toasted almonds

Soak raisins in sherry to cover them, fifteen minutes or longer. Heat
the oil in a skillet. Brown the meat in the oil then transfer it to a
Dutch oven. Add the onions and garlic to the skillet and cook,
stirring, until onions are wilted. Add the onions to the meat. Add
salt, red pepper flakes and the tumeric and stir. Add the raisins,
tomatoes, and enough chicken stock to cover.

Bring to a boil, then cover and simmer one and one half hours adding
more stock if necessary. Serve garnished, if you wish with almonds
and fried onion rings. This serves about 6 people.

Bstilla

This is a popular and very tasty pigeon pie which is often served for special guests.   Usually it will be a very large pie baked in an oversize utensil. The pie crust is so difficult to make that even the natives often use the fila pastry which is pre-prepared and can be procurred in most Greek groceries.

```
Take:  2 or 3 large pigeons or 4 smaller ones
       2 to 3 tablespoons of butter
       some salt and pepper
       chop up one large onion very fine
       a pinch or more of saffron
       1/2 teaspoon ground ginger
       1/2 teaspoon all spice
       3/4 teaspoon cinnamon
       1 tablespoon white sugar
       1/4 cup chopped fresh parsley
       1 handful of chopped almonds which have been fried
        quickly in butter
       9 eggs (one will be the yolk only which is beaten)
       10 tablespoons of salted butter melted
       About 15 sheets of fila
```

Cut the washed and cleaned pigeons in quarters (or halves if they are very small) and cook over a low heat for two hours in a kettle in a little water in which you have put some butter, onions and seasonings. They must be cooked until very tender. More water can be added if it cooks away.   Drain and save the juice. Take all the bones and skins away and cut up the meat in small pieces. Now beat the eggs and mix in the juice which you have saved, add a little salt and pepper and cook this slowly over the fire until it becomes thick and cream-like.

Rub some butter all over the inside of a pan which you can put in the oven.   This pan should be about 12 or 14 inches round and about 2 inches deep.   Put one sheet of fila in this with the ends folded up and over the top toward the outside of the pan. You may use two sheets if one is too small. Now add five more sheets, one on top of the other and brush melted butter between each sheet. On the top layer sprinkle the sugar and cinnamon and almonds. Put about 1/2 of the egg mixture on this, arranging it smoothly and moisten with some of the rest of the juice. Cover it with 3 or 4 sheets of fila dusting like before with melted butter. Now put the pieces of meat on it and cover this with what is left of the egg mixture. Cover with the last of the juice. Cover everything with the last fila sheets and put all edges over the top sheet closing all inside carefully. The beaten egg yolk can be dusted over the top to form a glaze. Bake for 40 minutes at 375° then turn heat up to 425° for 15 minutes. Be sure the pastry gets gold colored and is crisp, not soggy. Serve while very hot.

NETHERLANDS

The Netherlands, also known as Holland, is a comparatively flat country, much of which is below the level of the sea. The land was reclaimed from the water by the world famous Dutch dikes. The capital is Amsterdam, but the seat of the government is The Hague. The religions are the Dutch Reformed Protestant, Roman Catholic and Protestant Calvinist. The official language is Dutch. History shows the early tribes to have been Germanic, one of which was Batavi and which never capitulated to Julius Caesar's army. Rule has changed from Charlemagne's to the House of Burgundy, the Hapsburgs and Spanish domination until the Dutch revolt. Bicycling in this friendly and interesting country is a pleasant way to see it.

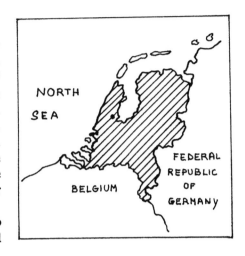

When guests are invited to dine they are expected to arrive on time or about five to ten minutes early or late. Guests may bring flowers to the hosts. Usually the host will greet you at the door and escort you to the living room for cocktails, wine, liquor, or schnapps which will be served with hors d'oeuvres. About one half hour will be spent visiting and if toasts are offered the expressions will be "Prost" or "Guzontite". Then all will go to the dining room where the table may be any shape, covered with a cloth and with cloth napkins and the usual silverware. Grace may be said or one may say "Bon appetit". A good rule to follow is to keep your hands on the table, even the one you may not be using to eat with.

The host will probably sit at one end of the table, if it is oblong, but seating varies. The hostess and guests may sit anywhere. Children may eat with the group, or if there are too many for one table they may sit at another one nearby. The meal may start with soup, often tomato, chicken or variations. There will also be meat or fish and potatoes, sometimes rice, vegetables and salad with a pre-mixed dressing. The food may be passed at the table. It is best not to offer to help if this is your first visit. For beverage there may be wine, water or nothing. Dessert may consist of chocolate pudding, ice cream, or fresh fruit. There will be much conversation.

In the villages the customs are more traditional; this will be in farming areas where all eat in the large kitchen area or adjacent alcove. Usually there will be one large dish and everyone helps himself. Here schnapps, beer or milk are used more than wine. In the winter the food will be a big stew type of dish and in the summer it may be separate dishes, potatoes, vegetables and meat. Guests can always offer to help and all is warm and very friendly.

After the meal the group will return to the living room where coffee and sometimes after-dinner drinks of liquor, etc., will be served. One should stay from one half hour until about 10 p.m., which is a normal leaving time as a rule, but one may stay longer depending upon the circumstances. Sometimes the host will hint at the time to leave by serving coffee a second time however, not everyone does this.

Always say the food is good and the word of thank you is "Dankuwell", pronounced dankewell. Do not send your hosts a thank you note, or gift, or telephone them, and do not invite them to your hotel for a meal, but if you insist, it is best to invite them to a restaurant. However, do invite them to visit you in your country and write them when you return to your home and repeat your thanks and invitation.

NICARAGUA

Nicaragua is the largest Central American country and its capital is Managua. The people are mostly Mestizo, a mixture of Spanish and Indian, with some Negro and pure Indian. The language is Spanish. The religion is Roman Catholic, although there is a freedom of religion and some of the Indians still practice their tribal customs. The climate is tropical and there are two great lakes, one of which has fresh water sharks. Columbus sailed along the coast in 1502 and the country soon after came under Spanish rule as did all Central America. In 1838 it became independent.

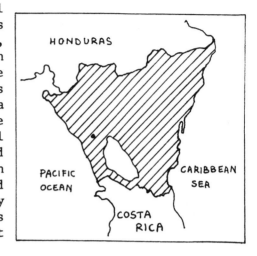

Preceding the arrival of the Spaniards, there were several Indian tribes living in Nicaragua. In the north and west, where there was much gold the inhabitants were hunters. In the northeast there were primitive Indians known as the Mosquito tribe. These lived along the Mosquito coast and many still live in this area today. Nicarao ruled the most powerful tribe which lived on the shore of Lake Nicaragua. These were peaceful agricultural people. There are carvings and glyphs on an island in the lake which have never been deciphered, but which show that there were once temples of high priests in the country and it is believed that this was a highly civilized Indian population. During the Spanish conquest many of these leaders were killed and much of their culture disappeared forever.

When you are invited to dinner in someone's home you should arrive around five minutes later than the time stated. It is not customary to bring flowers or a gift. The host and the hostess will greet you and you will visit for about one half hour in the living room. You probably will be offered a beverage or an alcoholic drink but it usually is not accompanied by hors d'oeuvres.

In the more modern home the dining room is separate whereas in the more traditional home they are one in the same. Children from the age of six often will eat with the group and most families will say Grace. The host begins eating in order to make the guests feel at ease. Generally serving dishes will be on the table and most families will have servants. Sometimes the food may be passed by those who are eating. A meal may include thick soup, salad and the main dish. The salad is served with the meal if there is soup, if not, the salad is served first, then the main dish. Usually this is roast beef but there may be pork or chicken and often fish. Occasionally there will be fried onions in it and many vegetables. The beverage may be fruit juices and sometimes wine or iced plain water. "Fresco de frutas" is a delicious mixed fruit drink made of tropical fruits. Usually tortillas, but sometimes bread, accompany the meal. The dessert may be bread soaked in rum or pudding, "Otolillo". Not much coffee is used but it may be offered to guests.

The conversation is plentiful and pleasant. One should compliment the food. After the meal, in the living room, one may remain up to a maximum of about two and one half hours. "Muchas gracias" are the words for thank you very much. It is not customary to send a gift or note or flowers but it is polite to telephone when you are leaving the country and to send a card or letter from your home when you return.

Baho

1 1/2 pounds beef	3 tomatoes
2 green bananas (plantain)	1 green pepper
3 yellow bananas (plantain)	2 onions
3 pieces of yuca	Salt (to taste)

Put inside a pot that has a "tapesco" in the bottom, with the three yellow bananas cut in half, with all of the peel. Peel off the two green bananas, cut them, and put the pieces inside the pot; on top of this put the beef which you prepare one day before you cook it. To prepare the beef, leave it under the sun with a lot of salt on it. Before you are going to cook it wash the salt off. Now add the yuca, which has been cut in medium sized pieces. Cut tomatoes, onions, and green pepper in round slices, add a little salt and cover everything with banana leaves. Leave the Baho on the fire for 2 1/2 to 3 hours. Check it periodically to see if it has enough water.

A tapesco is made by placing some sticks in the bottom of a pot to form a trellace-like stand. Fill to the top of the wood sticks and cover this with banana leaves--as though you were making a tray, as you might spread a sheet on a table, flattening the leaves so that they are level. This should not take up too much space, but be high enough to get a least two cups of water or more under the leaves.

NIGERIA

Lagos, the capital, is a city to which people come from all parts of Nigeria. The country is on the west African coast and its climate varies from hot and humid swamplands to tropical rain forest to dry semidesert. Nigeria has the largest population of the African countries approaching 70 million. There is a multitude of customs and languages and types of people including 250 ethnic groupings. Therefore it is impossible to describe what a visitor might find, but a general rule to remember is that it is easy to ask questions and learn the differences as one generally feels

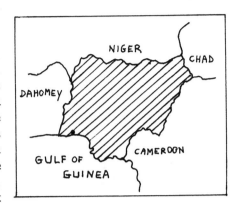

comfortable. The religions are mainly Muslim and Christian. Nigeria is an old country with an eventful recorded history dating to 1100 A.D. The official language is English and others are Hausa, Yoruba and Ibo. Its independence was achieved in 1960.

Muslims usually have three wives, or more if they can afford to take care of them. Most families are large, with fifteen or twenty children who are bound together by close family relations. Couples or families do not live in a house which has been lived in previously but always build their own.

Women are subservient to men in essentially all ways. If a man asks a wife to do something she automatically obeys. However, she is the director of the kitchen which is her place and she controls it completely. If her husband wishes more food and she says no, he will not contradict her. Usually a wife has one or more servants to help her with the preparation of foods.

For dining, there is a mixture of old and new customs. Some eat with fingers but others use the more common western style utensils. In traditional style only the righthand is used and rice may be eaten with a spoon as it is cooked to a soft consistency. In most areas chairs will be used, but in the North, a Muslim region, one sits on the floor on mats. The food is served on platters on the floor and all eat from the same dish. Usually a dinner will be at about 7 in the evening or later. Guests usually arrive about one half hour after the time for which they were invited and no gifts or flowers are brought to the hosts. Guests usually do not knock at the door but simply walk in and make themselves at home. It is only the foreigner who may hesitate to enter without permission. At the door anyone in the family may greet you and escort you to a living room. Seating will be western style and nothing wil be served (water may sometimes be offered, sometimes with ice, but no tea or coffee) as this is a time purely for talking. Any subject may be discussed and often this includes current affairs and always some remarks about the family, asking about their children, etc. This will be about a half hour visit. A bowl of water will be brought in by the hostess to wash hands which are always washed in front of guests.

In the dining room the table will be set with a cloth, white or colored, napkins and the usual silverware. The host sits at the head of the table, the hostess at the opposite end, and the guests on the sides. However, it is not unusual to have the host and hostess sitting together. The host leads a prayer and if there is no father or host, the hostess will ask another man to say it. It can be of any religion or something made up for the occasion. The food will already be on the table and the host will begin to eat first. Meals may consist of roasted meat, beef, fowl, lamb, etc., soup with meat and vegetables in it and the vegetables may be yams, yam porridge, or yams dipped in palm oil, and bread and butter. Fruits, eaten with fingers at all times may be oranges, paupa, bananas, mangos, guavas or avocados. If using the fingers the soup is eaten with yams or rice or a cassaba tuber, ground like flour and used to sponge up the soup. Dinner conversation is abundant and you may ask to help, compliment the food, or ask for a recipe. Hands are washed in the dining area before the guests return to the living room. Here drinks are served which may include beer and whiskey. In the Muslim area religion prohibits pork and liquor. Here mineral water and tea are served. A guest may sit for a long time and talk until he thinks the discussions have ended. This is a time to relax.

When leaving you may simply say thank you for the dinner and the evening. No notes are sent, nor gifts nor flowers. Your host will probably escort you for a long distance from his door and you will feel that he wishes to prolong the friendship. It is polite to call and say goodbye a day or two before you leave the country and then you may write from home telling about your voyages as your hosts will like to hear from you.

Fu Fu (A very popular food)

This can be mashed cooked yam with no flavoring. It is used with soup and swallowed without chewing.

You may use Bisquick or farina. Boil water in a pot and when it is boiling, add the farina by scooping up a handful and with fingers outstretched, scatter it on top of the water in a circular motion, as you might scatter seeds. When the mixture begins to thicken, stir vigourously until it is very stiff. Next, drop it all onto a large plate. To eat it take some with your fingers (right hand only) dip it into soup and toss it into your mouth. There is no salt or other flavoring added to Fu Fu and you must judge for yourself the quantity of farina to use for a thick consistency.

Soup

Use meat, fish, peanuts or egusi (like melon seeds). Add vegetables which you wash and palm oil, salt, pepper, and onions. Boil all together for a long time.

Kola

This is a fruit which is eaten before dining. The owner of the house brings the kola in his hands and presents it to the guest. The symbol is one of mutual friendship. A prayer is said, using the kola, with the thought that it is eaten in the honor of the ancestors for long life and prosperity. It is supposed to help the guest and the host to have a long life (life expectancy in Nigeria is very short) and it is for each other. The host hands the kola, which is about the size of a cup, to the guest for him to see it, then the guest hands it back to the host. The women do not enter into this ritual which is called breaking kolas. The host breaks off a piece, and gives it back to the guest and they eat it together.

A sojourn in Nigeria will be filled with interesting discoveries if the traveler is curious and receptive.

PAKISTAN

Pakistan was known as West Pakistan when
its counterpart, Bangladesh, was East
Pakistan. Its capitol is Islamabad but
many visitors will recognize the city of
Karachi more readily because this is the
city most usually visited. Karachi is a
major city near the Arabian sea while
Islamabad is in the north of the country
not far from Kashmir in India. The
people are Punjabi, Sindhi, Pushtun and
Baluchi. The religion is almost totally
Muslim with some Christian and Hindu.
The official language is Urdu and other
languages are English, Punjabi, Sindhi,
Pushtu and Baluchi. The temperature in

Pakistan can vary from freezing to 120° F. Although the country is
one of the present century, its recorded history dates to the seventh
century when Muslim sailors arrived and captured some of its
territory. After the Afgans and Turks invaded the area and Britain
became involved in the 1800's. At one time Pakistan was to have been
established as a homeland for the Muslims of the sub-continent. The
country gained its independence in 1947.

In Pakistan, one may be invited for dinner or lunch. You should
arrive from ten minutes to one half hour later than the hour for which
you were invited, unless you are told to "be on American or British
time", which means you should be prompt. Do not bring flowers or a
gift. In a conservative family, the hostess will not greet you at the
door as this is done by the host. However, this custom is changing in
many areas as the country becomes more modernized. In the more
liberated, usually the upper class, any one or all may greet you. You
should shake hands as it is considered rude not to do so when you
arrive. There is much body contact between people and more among the
men than is usual in the United States.

In the living room, a pre-dinner visit will be about one half hour.
Usually nothing will be served during this time. The host will lead
the guests to the dining room where the seating is informal as a
general rule and even the host may not always sit in the same place at
each meal. In the cities forks are used but in the villages people
eat with their fingers. The meal may begin with rice or a hotly
spiced curry dish, often with chicken, barbecued or roasted.
"Biryani" is a main dish of rice, meats, vegetables and curry. Bread
is called "Pratha" or "Roti" and is used, held between the fingers, to
eat with if utensils are not available. Beverages may be cold drinks,
Coca-Cola, juices, milk or water. Wine may be served in upper class
modern families. At the beginning of a meal one says, "Bismillah",
which means, "We begin in the name of God". If you do not like the
food you may say so politely, and you will not be expected to eat it.

It may be too hot for you. Naturally, your hosts would be more pleased if you say you like it and at least try to eat most of it.

In the villages, all men eat together and as most live in small houses, the women will be in a separate house cooking the foods and working at domestic chores. Usually you will not even see the women who may often be in purdah. Because it is believed sinful for any part of a woman's body to be seen by any man other than her husband, she wears a garment which covers her from head to toe, exposing only her eyes and hands. There are special ways to wrap the purdah garment and draping is carefully planned for comfort and concealment. A young girl must learn to drape her purdah from other women, as she learns most customs and household duties. Women gather together in groups and assist each other in these learning processes and traditions are passed down from generation to generation. Therefore, it is often difficult for a woman from the western world to become acclimated to the Pakistani way of life; few books can explain the intricate pattern of the day to day activities of the ladies. They must be learned by observation and personal conversations, and only in the native tongue can they be truly interpreted. A foreign woman may feel like an outsider in spite of the fact that the native women are dear to her and try in every way to make her feel at home.

In these homes you always eat with your fingers. In keeping with the Islamic faith villagers sit on the floor and the food is served on the floor. There will be curry, fish, lamb or beef. No pork nor ham nor bacon is eaten in Pakistan. This also comes from the Islamic religion. After fruit or almond cakes, which may end the meal, everyone says, "Shukar al Hamdulilah", "Thank you God for the food". Hands are washed again at this time. When they are washed before the meal there was no towel for drying as the towel might contaminate them whereas this time they will be towel dried. There will be a small basin for this just outside of the dining area. The washing of hands is an important custom and is even taught in the schools.

Pasanda Curry

For about six to eight people cut
  2 1/2 pounds of cube steak into 3/4"
  strips
2 cups yogurt
1 cup oil
5 or cardamons
5 or 6 peppercorns

4 red chiles, dried
8 cloves garlic, cut

1 piece ginger, fresh, about 2",
  sliced
1 onion, sliced

First fry onions in oil until they are a golden color and then add all
other items.   Cook over a low heat until the meat is tender and the
oil separates, keeping the fire low enough not to burn.

Firini

This is a very popular dessert which is a pudding that tastes
something like soft cookies. It has in it cream of rice and milk and
some pistachio nuts among other things.

There is a great variety of dishes and eating in Pakistan can be an
interesting and pleasant adventure.

PERU

Lima, the capital of Peru is a city with modern and old buildings and it has the largest Chinatown in the world, except for San Francisco's. It is also the city from which visitors take the plane to fly to the city of Cusco and then the road to Machu Pichu, the famous Indian ruins on the mountain top. From Lima the people must go to the nearby city of Chosica in order to see the sun in winter because the sky is continually over-cast with a layer of clouds during Peru's winter season. However, it is not very cold and there is no rain. Ancient Inca artifacts, including such

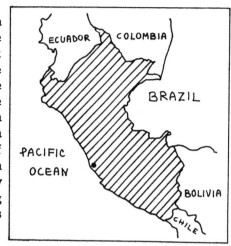

items as feathers which were used for ceremonial capes or string fish net pieces may be found lying on the earth to this day, still intact. These have not deteriorated due to rainfall and moisture or other natural elements. The sun may have parched them, but no water has hastened their decay. Water must be brought into the lowlands from mountains and is carried in stone aqueducts built by the early Indian inhabitants.

The climate of the country varies because of the coast, the mountains and jungle areas. In the Amazon River, at the city of Iquitos one finds beautiful light-colored fresh water dolphin. The people are mostly descendents of the Inca or pre-Inca Indians and some are Mestizos and Caucasians. The religion is Roman Catholic and the official language is Spanish but many Indians speak only Quechua or Aymara. Some of these Indians live in a lifestyle of long ago. The story of the Incas is interesting and tragic. After the Inca rule, which was very highly civilized, Peru came under the rule of Spain finally and achieved free independence in 1824.

In Peru bullfighting is a traditional and popular sport called: "Corrida de Toros". This differs from the bullfights in other Latin American countries because the bullfighters perform on horseback instead of on foot. October is the most festive bullfighting season during which time religious processions (the most famous being the procession of "Senor de los Milagros") last for five days or more.

Cock fighting or "Pelea de Gallos" is another popular sport at which betting is extremely heavy, especially within the social groups in the provinces outside of Lima.

Both these sports may be difficult for a visitor to enjoy as the animals and the fowls are the victims. However, the graceful passes of a good bullfighter can be appreciated for their excellence of balance and art, and visitors who study or follow the fights learn to recognize the finer aspects of these movements and may well become addicted to the sport.

Over the mountains and down into the jungle area of Peru, a visitor finds the city of Iquitos where the Amazon makes a large curve which is used as a harbor for shipping. You may take a ship from here all the way to the ocean, about a fourteen day trip through the jungle river where few people have travelled. There are tropical fruits and jungle animals but the trip is hot and humid and not everyone will enjoy the weather. In the harbor of Iquitos there are fresh water white dolphins which swim near the boats and play in sheer joy; which are fascinating to see. This little city also has swallows which arrive at five or six o'clock each evening. It is a city filled with nature, near to the original, and still inhabited Indian dwellings. It is unlike the Lima area in every way and is worth a trip if you are curious about the variety of life in Peru.

The Peruvian dinner hour is about 9 or 9:30 in the evening and you should arrive about one half hour later than your invitation states. Guests may bring a bottle of wine, liquor or chocolate, but not flowers. The host and hostess often greet guests at the door although most families have servants. In the living room cocktails are served and these will usually be the traditional Pisco Sour. Guests sometimes visit here for up to two hours while sharing conversation, drinks and hors d'eourves. At the dining table the host and hostess often sit near each other and the hostess may use a small table on wheels nearby from which she serves the guests. Seating is very informal and families usually do not say Grace. The host serves the wine and the hostess takes care of the food unless there are young girls in the family who may help. There is a cloth, napkins, and the usual silverware. One may use the fork in the right hand. The host will begin to eat first. There may be soup, but usually there is a salad or a shrimp cocktail followed by the main dish which may be fish, chicken or meat. Rice is served with the meal and there may also be potatoes at the same time along with other vegetables. All salt things are removed from the table before dessert. Ice cream, rice puddings or little cakes and rather mild coffee end the meal. There is much conversation about many subjects and one should compliment the food. Often all will sit at the table after the meal for a long time while talking. "Salud" is the word one uses to offer a toast to someone's health. After returning to the living room you should remain at least one half hour and leave at 10:30 or 11 p.m. and no later than twelve o'clock if the next day is a working day.

"Mushas gracias" is thank you very much. No note or gift need be sent but you should telephone to say goodbye and then write from your home if you wish.

Pisco Sour (Pisco is a grape brandy and can be bought in some liquor stores)

You will need some cracked ice, about 6 jiggers of Pisco to one jigger of simple syrup (water and sugar), the juice of one large lemon (or about 2 to 3 tablespoons), a few shakes of bitters, an egg white. Mix the Pisco and syrup, juice and bitters in a cocktail shaker and then add the finely cracked ice and egg white and shake well and pour immediately.   It should look frothy and is delicious, but it may be stronger than it seems when you taste it.

Anticuchos

Take one beef heart and cut in small pieces, about one cup of vinegar with taragon in it, about a small teaspoon, or 1/2 teaspoon of ground chili pepper and a large pinch of saffron, 3 pieces of chopped garlic, about 10 peppercorns, a teaspoon of salt and 1/4 cup olive oil, and about 1/4 cup of water. Remove skin from heart and cut into small pieces.   Mix everything together except the meat and the oil. Then put the meat into the mixture and let it soak overnight to marinate it.   Put the meat pieces on skewers and roll them in a flat dish in the oil, then broil them until they are tender, adding the sauce in which they were marinated over them. Many Peruvians barbeque this very popular dish which sometimes is eaten with corn on the cob.

PONAPE

Ponape is an island in the archipelago known as the Caroline Islands and it is a Trust Territory of the United States. Here there is a natural beauty with coral reefs, clear water and gentle people with a simple way of life. The harmonious life of the natives has often been harassed by military invasion but there are still some ruins of a culture which dates back to centuries ago. The natives are Micronesians and their customs are interesting, and though simple sometimes show a great insight into the manner in which people might live together peacefully. The weather is balmy and life has a natural feeling.

There is a saying in Ponape that early time is Ponape time and late time is American time. When you are invited for dinner you should arrive about five or ten minutes early. It is not necessary to bring a gift but you may bring toys for the children if you wish. Any member of the family may greet you and escort you to the living room where you will sit for a few moments and then be asked if you wish something to drink. Any member of the family may greet you and escort you to the living room where you will sit for a few moments and then be asked if you wish something to drink. The beverages may be cocktails but with a special meal you may be offered "Gava". This is made from plants, trunk and root pounded on a stone and hibiscus bark is squeezed so that all these juices go together. It is a very strong drink and one may get drunk quickly from it. It will be served in a small coconut shell. The host will offer it to you, you then take a sip and offer it back to your host. The guest sips first. Then it is passed around and after about two people sip it is passed back and re-filled. There is usually no food served with this. You may spend about one half to two hours drinking and talking. If anything is served with Gava it is either sweet or hot and some people prefer water with sugar along with it to remove the strong taste. While drinking, the host will ask the guests if they wish to continue to drink or to stop now and eat. Before eating the hands are washed in a washroom or at an outside faucet or a bowl in the same room. There will be a bar of soap and a towel.

The meal will be eaten in the same room and all go to a table or sit on a mat and eat on the floor. There will be the usual cutlery and plates, salt and hot pepper and usually some shoyu sauce. Christians often say Grace before the meal, other families do not. There will be many dishes and these are usually placed in a row down the center of the table or floor mat. Many tables have benches attached to them.

The host sits at one end and the hostess at the other, guests at the sides. There will be a cloth and napkins at the table. The seating arrangement will be the same on the floor mats, but here one sits with feet crossed in front and knees over heels, women may sit with feet to the side, knees bent. Water is the only beverage at the meal. There may be fish, beans, potatoes, vegetables, salad and no bread. The host helps himself and then passes the dish, each helps himself with the wooden serving spoon. When the dishes are finished you will be asked if you wish coffee or tea or Ponapean "mateu", which is a tree bark, cleaned inside and out and put into boiling water. When it boils the water becomes bright red. It is usually drunk hot with sugar. It is healthy and good for an upset stomach. There will be no fruit as bread and fruits are eaten during the morning, not in the evening. Fish may be broiled, fried, roasted or sashimi, which is raw with salt, pepper, and lots of lime juice mixed well together. The fish is soaked in this juice. There is no conversation while eating. After the meal conversation may be about any subject but it should be pleasant. The host will ask if you wish anything else and you should tell him that you like the food. A guest may leave at any time. If the host must start to work early the next morning you should leave soon after eating.

MAT

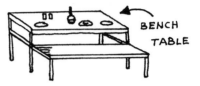

BENCH TABLE

The word for thank you is "Kalanan". You may send a gift if you wish or you may invite your hosts to your hotel for a meal. It is customary to call or telephone before leaving and to write when you return to your country.

There is a banana and rice dish which is made of ripe banana, and rice which is cooked together then mashed and served with coconut oil and salt on it. The coconut oil is made from powdered and squeezed coconut meat.

SAIPAN

Saipan is one of the Mariana Islands in
the Pacific Ocean.   It is small and
hilly. These islands were discovered by
Magellan in 1521 and were under the rule
of Spain, Germany, Japan and now are a
trust territory of the United States.
Because of their strategic position they
have seen bitter fighting in the past
but their people are friendly and
hospitable.

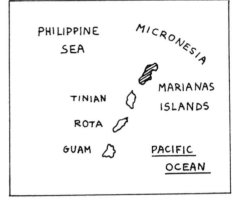

When you think of the gentle natives on
the islands in this part of the Pacific
Ocean, and when you realize that these
people for centuries had their own
laws, their own ways of life, their own beliefs which blended
particularly well with their geographical setting, and when they went
from one island to a neighboring one they communicated well and often
lived together as friends, you must begin to doubt whether the various
bits of modern civilization brought to them has been a blessing or a
hindrance. The islands in general have been sought after, fought over
and neglected in varying degrees by various nations and their people
have had little to say about any of these cycles. Hardly ever has the
native philosophy been recognized, let alone appreciated. Presently a
number of students are coming to the mainland of the United States to
study and enhance their skills in trades with the assurance they will
find useful places in their society when they return. These students
often reflect their inherited customs--they make friends easily and
are curious about other ways of living, but at all times seem anxious
to return to their beloved island where they can "relax" and enjoy
life as it comes to them in a truly natural way. They dread wars,
having been helpless pawns in them--"where could we run? Where could
we hide? Why did our land have to suffer so?", they asked after World
War II.   They had no fair chance as they were literally trapped
between the fury of great nations at war with all the modern equipment
tearing at them day and night. They seek a peaceful life among their
friends and relatives to whom they feel very close. They are a gentle
people who want you to be happy on their island.

One usually is invited for dinner at 6 o'clock and the dinner will
probably be at about 7. You may arrive about fifteen minutes early or
a little late, but it is best to be early. You may bring flowers to
your hosts, or a gift from your country, but no food. The host and
hostess or just the hostess may greet you and escort you to the living
room where there will be western type furniture. The culture of
Saipan resembles that of Europe or America. You will visit for about
one half hour or more while you are offered tea, coffee, wine, hard
drinks or soft drinks which will be accompanied by hors d'oeuvres or
snacks.   Before dinner you will wash your hands in a guest room. The

hostess will usually lead the guests to the dining room. At the table the host will sit at one end and the hostess at the other and guests at the sides. Usually children sit at a separate table. There will be a cloth, glasses, plates, fork, knife and spoon, and coffee cups on the table.

Wine and rolls with butter are served. The meal may consist of salad, soup, meat (often steak), chicken (often roasted), mashed or baked potatoes, pies and fruits. Tropical fruits are eaten with a knife and fork but papaya is eaten with a spoon. Coffee will be offered with sugar and cream and is referred to as "light" or "dark" coffee. After the meal the host will toast the guests and all will leave the dining room. In the living room you may remain for up to four hours while visiting and you may be asked to spend the night.

A thank you upon leaving and a compliment for the food are customary. Thank you notes are not sent. Your hosts may give you a gift as a souvenir of Saipan and you should not send a gift to them. You may invite your hosts to have dinner with you at your hotel but they more than likely will turn the tables and invite you for a picnic on the beach. A letter from home when you return will be appreciated.

SAMOA

Pago Pago harbor in Samoa is one of the most beautiful harbors in the world. Although American, Samoa is like a foreign country to the United States visitor.   It became of interest to the United States Navy in the 1800's because of its geographical position related to shipping.   The people had a very cooperative and complex set of customs. There was always enough food as one could simply gather it from wild growth and the people had a very relaxed way of living. The social system was basically that of the extended family and to this day the clan chief is important.

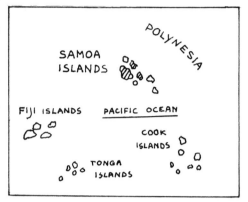

Thatched houses were used for living and for schools. The Samoan language was first written by American Christian missionaries, mainly to translate the Bible. The religions are Catholic, Mormom and other Christian sects. There is a mixture of native Samoans, mixed whites, and whites who came with the Naval governors and the missionaries. America's history in Samoa is sketchy and lax, but the Samoans date back many centuries and are a pleasant, relaxed people. Samoan money merits special mention. Samoans much prefer the visitor to use native money other than currency which the visitor brings from his homeland. It is considered much more respectable to use the local money which is woven mats. These are woven by women, are very beautiful and can have designs with feathers in them. One mat about three, four, or five feet by three feet will be the equivalent of about $10.

Usually dinner will be at about 8 o'clock and you should be on time. You may bring a gift to the family if you wish.   There may or not be three meals a day in Samoa. Sometimes there is only one but everyone eats the native fruits at any time. The host will greet you but there is no actual door. Your hosts will watch for your arrival and will be freshened to welcome you. The family Chief will say "Matai", which means this is your home just as it is my home, please make yourself at home.   The home will be a hut with no rooms and open to the outside with posts to support its thatched roof. The hostess quickly puts down clean fresh mats for you to sit on. All sit in front of the house with knees folded to the side as in Yoga position, feet crossed in front.   The food is prepared in the rear. All sit for about five minutes and then a bowl of water, soap and a towel will be brought for you to wash your hands. Then a woven lau lau leaf tray is brought to you. This will be covered with banana or grape fruit leaves and on it is some cooked taro root, bananas, cooked fish and coconut milk. There will also be "Palusami" which is made with coconut milk, taro leaves and onions and salt and cooked in an oven or "umu" with hot coals. Three leaves are folded into a cup shape and drawn together at the top for filling it with coconut milk. Then a banana leaf is wrapped around that and a bread fruit leaf is tied around it using the end of the stem to clasp it together. The milk inside becomes firm as ice cream. This is cooked about 45 minutes in an umu or hot oven. Also roast pig may be served cut in special pieces. This is eaten with fingers or a fork. The pig may be roasted whole and pre-cut. Each piece has a name given to it. The leg is for the Chief, another leg for the guest, etc., and the head is for the servants, ribs are for a minister or pastor. Fruit is not eaten at meals as it is eaten so often during the day, except for melons. These are cut with a knife and eaten with fingers. There are plates and in the more modern homes there are tables and chairs and regular utensils. The Chief will say Grace and he will begin to eat.

Each family has a Chief and each Chief has a servant who can be his son, a daughter, a husband, or another relative. When the Chief dies his servant takes the Chief's place and becomes the new Chief. In Samoa a Chief should always have a servant. When the Chief pushes his tray away from him the bowl of water for washing hands will be offered again. Conversation is customary all through the meal. Beverages may include water, soft drinks, hard liquor (sometimes before and after the meal), strong coffee and tea for older people and weak coffee and especially weak tea for the young. Coca-Cola is very popular and whiskey and beer and sometimes mixed drinks are used.

After the meal one should stay until about 11 or 12 or later depending upon the circumstances. Always compliment the food when thanking your hosts. You may invite your hosts to your hotel for a meal to reciprocate if you wish. It is customary to drop by and thank them again and it is very polite to write a letter when you return to your home.

SAUDI ARABIA

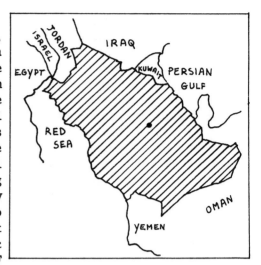

Saudi Arabia has three capitals: Riyadh, Jiddah (the diplomatic capital) and Mecca (the religious capital). The people are of Arab tribal descent with some from other Arab countries including some Muslims. The main religion is Sunni Islam and the language is Arabic. It has a monarchist government and since the discovery and development of its oil resources, it is a constantly changing nation. It is a large country, mainly desert, with some areas too dry to sustain human life. It has no permanent rivers or lakes and very erratic rainfall. The climate varies from 120° F and humid in some areas, to occasionally below freezing in the central and northern parts. Although this area of the world has been populated for centuries, Saudi Arabia was only established as a country in 1932 by King Abd al-Aziz.

A little known fact is that a great part of eastern Saudi Arabia was at one time under water. There were seas which were filled with marine life this is the area where much of the oil comes from today. The decomposed fish and plant life became petroleum under the pressure of layers of sand and mud. At present this area is dry and harsh, with little vegetation. Sand dunes are blown about in the strong winds and sometimes whole areas seem to shift as the sand moves from one place to another. At times whole villages have been covered in the storms. Airplanes can be grounded even in the more gentle storms and visitors should be aware of this before travelling in these areas.

Almost all of Saudi Arabia's income comes from oil and this has been used to develop schools, roads, deep water ports on the Red Sea, hospitals, railroads, and places for Pilgrims to stay when they visit Mecca. When visiting Saudi Arabia one must be ever conscious of changing customs.

The quest for education grew rapidly when the oil industry developed and many students are sent to other countries by the Saudi government in order to be trained in various fields. The natives realize that their country needs a variety of industries and social developments for the future. They are preparing their citizens for these opportunities.

Dinner may be from 5 to 9 o'clock and is often at 6. You may arrive up to a half hour early or 10 or 15 minutes late. Dinner will be served usually earlier in the winter months than in summer. You may bring your hosts a gift but usually this is not done and, in fact, the hosts sometimes have gifts for the guest. If you are husband and wife the female guest will probably join the women and the male will go with the men. There are two doors from which to greet guests. One is for females, who are met by a mother, wife, sister or other female relative and one door where men will meet the males. Even as this is written in some families now any member or all may greet any or all guests. (In the southern area customs are under Oriental influence and may differ from other sections; here no one is a guest except Muslims). Liquor is never used because of the religion, but tea is drunk all day. Sometimes nuts or seeds are served. Men often smoke and if they do they carry their own cigarettes. Women never smoke. You will wash your hands in a special annex or rest room and then you will enter a rug room where you will sit on pillows. There is no table and the platters are placed on the floor by brothers or men, the women do not do this although the women will have prepared the food. Before eating all day, "Bis m'Allah". The women will be in a separate room, talking, and they will enter the same rug room and eat when the men have finished. But, when guests are present the women will eat in another room entirely. Eating is done with fingers using the right hand only, although a guest may be asked if he would prefer a spoon or other utensil. The host and guest sit first and the oldest person begins to eat first. The meal may begin with dates and a plate of butter. You may slightly dip the edge of a date in the butter and eat it, or it may be eaten plain. If dipped, one eats only two or three dates. There will always be rice and this may be served with meat, fish, or fowl. If the meat is in large pieces, a novice at finger eating will probably need a knife. Soup is eaten with bread, sometimes a spoon is used and sometimes the soup is used as a sauce over the rice. Vegetables and salads and fruits, buttermilk and custard will round out the meal. Usually there are no cakes or cookies. Milk is drunk hot with sugar, never cold. There are no individual plates and all eat from the center dish. This, however, is changing in many homes. There will be no napkins and you will wash your hands again after the meal, and be offered cologne to freshen your skin. The host and guests always wash first. Now you will return to the sofa room where there may be strong coffee, served in a cup, or tea, served in a glass with a handle. Sometimes incense is offered and started by one of the men who uses it and passes it on. Each waves some on himself with his hands and passes it on to the person on his right. Guests may leave any time after the incense has been passed to the last person. It is polite to remain longer, especially if your host insists, which he usually does. And when he does, he is sincere. If you have come for lunch, however, do leave soon, as your hosts will wish to sleep. Ordinarily on should leave at about an hour after the meal.

"Shokran" is the word for thank you. Do not send flowers. You may send a thank you note or a small gift, but always call and say goodbye when you leave the country.

Kabsa

Use a pot over the fire, covered. Slice some onions and put into a pot with a little vegetable or corn oil. Cook until the onions are transparent. Add cut small meat pieces and water to cover meat (always keep meat covered). Add salt to taste. Add sliced tomatoes. Continue adding water to cover meat until tender. Then add raw rice and simmer until rice is dryish cooked. Also add some herbs: safron, mint and others depending upon what you wish. Salt and pepper can be added while eating.

SINGAPORE

Many people do not realize that Singapore, the city, is the capital of Singapore Island, the country. This whole country has only about one and one half million people but it is an important focal point for Asian sea routes, and the city gives one the feeling of over-population, as most of the island's people are centered there. The country is very low and includes some land which has been reclaimed from the sea. The weather is humid. The tropical fruits in this area of the world are prolific and delicious. Although there is religious freedom with

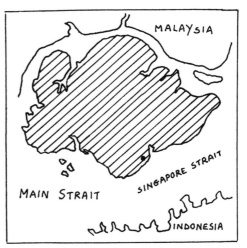

many Chinese faiths, almost all the Malays are Muslim and others are Hindus, Sikhs, Taoists, Buddhists, Confucianists and Christians.
The famous Sir Thomas Stamford Raffles from England, after whom one of the historical hotels is named, was influencial in the purchase of Singapore by Britain. For a short time under Japanese occupation in World War II and then connected again with Britain, the country became an independent Republic in 1965.

If you wish an adventure in eating, Singapore is the place. You may dine like a lord in an air conditioned, fully carpeted restaurant where you may have exquisite French cuisine and wine; or you may help yourself from a banana leaf piled high with curry and rice; or dine on a tatami (woven mat) with sizzling Japanese steak served by waitresses in kimonos; or enjoy succulent crabs and prawns on a beach near the water; or dine leisurely in a theater restaurant; or have a meal of noodles fried for five minutes (while you wait) at a makan (food) stall. You can find a different dish each day in this country of mixed cultures. There are at least six styles of Chinese cooking. Malay and Indonesian dishes are mainly of Sumatran origin known as Nas Padang. These dishes are usually very hot as they are spiced with chilli and peppers. Authentic Indian foods are available in restaurants and European foods are served in hotels and large restaurants. These may have been brought from every corner of Europe. Wines and the service at your table will be excellent. Floating restaurants are interesting and the food and wines will be good. Music is provided for dancing and in this setting, under the stars with the city in view, it will be an evening to remember.

Dinner is at about 7 in the evening but normally you will be invited to dine at a restaurant. It is not customary to bring a gift when you arrive, especially as you will probably meet at the restaurant and not at the home. Normally you will have a Chinese dinner. The beverages preceding the meal may be soft drinks or alcoholic beverages. Nuts and pickles are often served at this time.

The dining table is usually round. Soup is served from a bowl and a lazy-Susan, or rotating platter, will be in the center with bowls at each place for each person. Chopsticks and a ceramic spoon are used. Usually cold dishes are served first and you should use a serving spoon to help yourself. There often are eight or ten courses and it is wise not to eat too much at the beginning of the meal.

Noodles are often used in the place of rice in restaurants whereas in the home rice is almost always eaten with the meal. There will be tea during the dinner, but no bread. Conversation is continuous throughout the dinner.

One may thank the hosts upon leaving and no thank you note or gift are sent to them. You may invite them to visit when you leave the country and call to say goodbye.

In some instances if, as an example, you are a friend from school, you may be invited to the home. As some families use chopsticks only, it is wise to know how to use them. However, many families also use Western style utensils. In the home there will be a round table with the food placed on it and you should serve yourself. Foods are steamed, boiled or quick fried as they are in China. There may be beef, pork and chicken but not lamb, and no bread. For sweets there may be fruits, ice cream or almond jelly.

The important thing to remember at a meal with many courses is to take a little of each, eating more toward the end of the meal than at the beginning.

SOUTH AFRICA

The capitals of South Africa are Pretoria (the administrative capital), Cape Town (the legislative), and Bloemfontein (the judicial). The country has three varying types of customs relating to the Africans, Whites and Coloreds. There is also a minority of Asians. About half of the Africians of the homelands are animists, the other religions are Dutch Reformed, Anglican, Methodist, Presbyterian and Jewish. The languages are Afrikaans, Aulu, Tswana, Sotho and some others. South Africa became independent in 1961 but racial turmoil continues. The weather, the beauty, the changing countryside, the coastal section with its magnificent shells, and the flowers of South Africa are world famous. Almost all types of plant life flourish here. The history of Caucasion rule over the natives and of the abuse of them through the industrial development of the country is well-known. In this book there will be only a glimpse of the white English dining customs, although it is hoped that visitors will be able to see all parts of South Africa and to meet people of all ethnic groups. Visitors to South Africa often pass by the beautiful apple orchards which are harvested mainly to make beverages. Not far from Cape Town there is the country's largest apple juice business where six different kinds of apples are blended into either a sparkling juice, or a cloudy unsparkling one. Much of this is reduced for export especially to Hong Kong and the Arab countries. The owner of the industry is a European immigrant who has a declaration on his office wall which states that all on his estate enjoy equal rights and privileges and each is entitled to equal pay for equal work. The three main products are a clear juice like champagne, the cloudy Applemist, and the concentrate which is mixed with flavors of seven other fruits. No artificial sweetening or preservatives are added. The drinks are pure and healthy and you will enjoy their clean and natural taste.

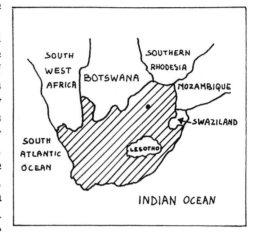

Dinner may be at about 5 in the evening and you should arrive on time. It is not customary to bring a gift to your hosts. The host usually will greet you and he and the hostess will escort you to the living room where you will visit for about on hour while having tea, or you may have cocktails with very light hors d'oeuvres. The conversation will cover many subjects and usually the guest is questioned by the hosts. When entering the dining room follow the hostess and she will indicate where you are to sit. Often the host and hostess sit at one end of the table together, or they may sit at opposite ends, with the guests at the sides. There will be a white cloth and, never paper, napkins--although the napkins are often in napkin rings. Two forks, two knives and two spoons will be at each place. Also there will be small bread and butter plates. Water or soft drinks are not served and the beverage will be wine or a continuation of the cocktail. Grace is said by the host. There is usually a maid who will bring in the main dish, often a roast. The host will carve this and pass a plate to each, guests first. Nothing but the meat is on the table at this time. After this is eaten, the host and hostess will pass other dishes, probably mashed potatoes, Yorkshire pudding and a vegetable. A guest does not ask for anything to be passed. Salads are usually only served with cold meats. Mint sauce, or jelly is served with lamb but no other jellies are used with meats. The maid will clear the plates from the table and bring in the dessert which may be tapioca pudding, cake or trifle. There are not many courses and the foods will be simply prepared, never hotly spiced. It is not customary to praise the food, especially since the servant probably will have prepared it.

When the meal is finished all will return to the living room where visiting will continue for up to one or two hours. When leaving it is customary to thank your hosts. Do be sure to send a thank you note immediately, but do not send flowers or a gift. You may call and invite your hosts to your hotel for lunch or dinner if you wish. A letter from your home after you have returned will be appreciated.

SRI LANKA

Sri Lanka, which is familiar to many
people by its former name of Ceylon, and
whose capital is Colombo, has a mixed
population of Burghers, Moors, Malays,
Sinhalese, Tamils, Europeans and
Veddahs. The religions are Buddhist,
Christian, Hindu and Islamic, and the
languages are Tamil, English, and
Sinhala which is the official language.
Sri Lanka has been independent since
1948, before which time rule was by
Sinhalese and others from India, Tamil,
some Portuguese, Dutch and British. The
climate is mostly tropical, but there
are high mountains where tea is grown.
Monsoons come in the early summer.

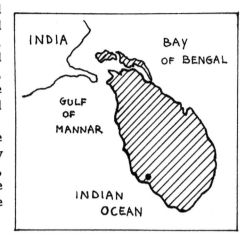

Dinners are from about 8:30 to 9 p.m. or later. When invited to a
home, a guest may arrive on time or a little later. Usually one
arrives about 7:30 or 8 and will eat at about 9 p.m. A late arrival
is quite usual, as one may arrive at 8:30 if invited to 8 p.m.
dinner.

The host and hostess may both greet and escort guests to the living
room which may have Western style furniture. Here cocktails are
served which may be alcholic (often wine), soft drinks, or fruit
juices with chips, hot hors d'oeurves, fried banana/chili chips, etc.
Anytime that all the guests have arrived, or in about one hour, they
will go to the dining room. The hostess is usually busy during this
pre-dinner time helping to, or preparing, the meal. Children may join
the group and often do for the dinner hour.

If the meal is in the traditional style and eaten with fingers, one
must wash hands before beginning. Sometimes fingers are used even if
there is cutlery or silverware on the table, sometimes only the
silverware is used, no fingers, but a fork and spoon only are used, no
knife. There may be water brought in bowls and placed at the side of
the table with soap and a towel, or guests may stop in the wash room
before entering the dining room. This all depends upon the individual
family.

The host will escort all to the dining area. The table may be round,
square, or oblong, with cloth and napkins. Seating is very informal
and you may sit anywhere. Often the host is at the head of the
table.The hostess does not sit and does not eat as she is busy looking
after the guests and she will eat later. Grace is often said by the
Christians, not by the Buddhists. Everyone begins by serving
himself.If there is rice and curry there will likely be no soup. The
salad is served with the rest of the meal. Salt, water, vinegar,

pineapple, tomatoes are arranged around a platter often mixed in sequence for design. Guests take what they want. The dessert may be fresh fruits, ice cream or pudding. If it is Western style, there may be soup, salad with dressing, usually steak as the main course, vegetables and dessert. If rice is eaten, a fork and spoon may be used, although many think it tastes better when eaten with fingers because it is easier to mix the various foods together. Fresh water is brought to replenish that at the side of the table, and hands are washed again. It is polite to comment about the food. Compliments are appreciated. Guests do not offer to help as there is almost always a servant to clear and clean the dishes after the meal.

After dinner a strong coffee is served in the living room. It is customary to remain here for at least one hour, and to leave before midnight, using one's good judgment. The opportunity to talk with the mother/hostess is at this time, after the meal.

The words for thank you are, "Bohoma stuthi" (pronounced stuti). You may invite your hosts to the hotel, telephone them, or write and say goodbye, then write from your homeland and invite them to visit. No other thanks is needed.

SWEDEN

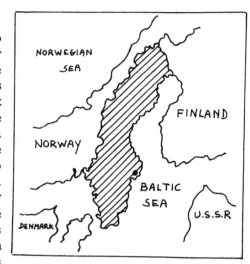

One of the countries which extends into the Arctic Circle, Sweden has a warmer climate than might be expected because of its location on the Gulf Stream. Its northern winters may last more than six months and it gets dark at 3 p.m. There are many forests and lakes but only a little arable land. Stockholm, the capital, is forever interesting to visitors with its modern architectural structures contrasting with older buildings, museums and homes. The people are homogeneous with minorities of Finns and Lapps. The state religion is Lutheran and the official language is Swedish. Christianity appeared during the Viking era and Sweden at one time included in its Baltic Empire both Finland and Norway. It is a constitutional monarchy, using a government adopted in 1809. In recent years the handcrafts of Sweden have become very popular. Visitors will find many objects from which to choose and it may be difficult to recognize the best purchase. There is a nation-wide Swedish handcraft organization which functions as follows: each county or administrative district has its own association and in some cases several. The association gives work only to people in the actual area and it acts as a sales organization for their work. There is a guarantee device which you can usually find on an item which is a round blue and yellow emblem with the words SVENSK SLOJD in white in the middle. This may be used only when an article has been inspected and approved by a jury of five impartial experts who are selected independently of the association itself. This jury is concerned only with wholesale and export goods. However, if you find something that you wish to buy, and you like it, do not hesitate to make the purchase, as there may be artifacts made locally for the local trade which have other marks on them.

Sweden feels that as long as people enjoy the right to make what they wish and the more machine-produced, often synthetic, goods that are manufactured, the more everyone shall learn to appreciate the natural, handmade things and the greater will become the pleasure over smooth fine textures of hand processed wood, linen, wool and other natural materials.

Dinner is at about 6 in the evening and you should arrive on time or about five minutes before the invitation, but never late. If you wish, you may bring your hostess flowers, chocolates or fruits, but not a permanent gift such as a book or a vase. Your host and hostess will greet you and lead you to the salon or living room where cocktails are being served. There probably will not be any hors d'oeuvres and you will visit here for about fifteen minutes to one half an hour. The hostess will announce when the dinner is ready and the host and hostess may both help in the kitchen and with the serving. You may offer to help but do not insist. Dining tables vary in shape and everyone sits where he/she wishes but you will be directed in order to make you feel at home. The utensils are the usual Western style silverware and the dishes will be passed at the table. Guests begin to eat first, but be aware that some families say Grace before the meal. There may be soup, and or a small salad with vinegar and oil dressing, probably roasted or boiled chicken, fish or meat, hard European style bread, butter and cheese. The salad is eaten at the same time as the main dish. Beverages may be beer, milk, fruit juices or schnapps. When drinking schnapps the glasses are raised and people say, "Skal". There is no dessert as a rule, at this time.

Conversation is plentiful and about all subjects. You should say that the food is good and you should eat everything on your plate. When finished, your silverware should be placed together on your plate; if

MEANS YOU WANT MORE

it is crossed it will mean that you wish to have more. You may have some dessert after have returned to the salon where mild coffee will be served. Cake or fruit will be offered with little plates and a napkin. You should remain from about forty-five minutes to two hours, depending upon the family.

WHEN FINISHED

"Tacksamycket" means thank you very much. No other thanks is needed. You may invite your hosts to a meal at your hotel or a restaurant, although this is not expected.

Finally, you should call or write when you leave Sweden and write again from your home when you have returned. It is an adventure to try the many different fish dishes in Sweden and you will surely enjoy them.

Sillpudding

8 fillets of salt herring
8 medium sized potatoes
1/4 cup chopped fine parsley (some people use dill)
5 onions
3 eggs
1/2 cup bread crumbs

3/4 of a cube of butter
2 cups milk
1/2 teaspoon pepper (black)

The herring must be soaked in clear water for about 8 hours. Change to fresh water and rinse the fish gently at least 3 times. Throw out the water and dry the fish, then cut it into thin strips. Slice the potatoes and onions very thin. Rub butter all over the inside of a casserole. Fill the casserole with layers of fish, potatoes and onions. Over each set of layers sprinkle the parsley. Do this until all the ingredients are used up. With a fork, whip the milk and eggs and pepper together well, and pour over the top. Cover this with the bread crumbs and the rest of the butter cut into little pieces. It should be baked for about 50 minutes at 350°. Serve very hot.

SWITZERLAND

Switzerland, often spoken of as the neutral country because of its stand during wars, is governed by Bern, a city which visitors enjoy. Geneva, another important city, has been and continues to be the focal point for many international organizations and world negotiations. The weather ranges from mild to very cold and permanently ice covered mountains may be seen. Switzerland is a small country and is often referred to as a picture post card country because of its natural beauty and its style of buildings. Its ethnic make up is Indo-European and its

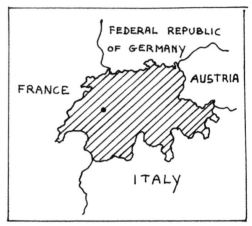

languages are German, French, Italian and Romansh; all of these are official languages. Romonsh is the minority language of the four, it has homewords of Latin or Italian origin, "ciao" is used as in modern Italian--only about 60,000 people speak it but it is their language. Swiss religions are Roman Catholic, Protestant and Jewish, with a scattering of others. Agriculture is important and Switzerland is famous for its cheese and sauces. The original inhabitants were Helvetic Celts, hence the name Helvetia which is used often for this country. Although Switzerland was a part of the Roman Empire, visitors do not go there to see Roman Ruins. After the Romans there were invasions by Teutonic tribes and Burgundians--there were many foreign influences. In 1848, a Federal Constitution was adopted. Visitors will find accommodations comfortable and fastidiously managed as the Swiss are famous for the hotel business. Students come from the world over to study this trade and the Swiss may be found in many other countries where they act as hotelkeepers. They are also famous as bankers, especially for their ability to handle investments frugally and secretively. Billions have been deposited in Swiss banks by kings, dictators, business tycoons, and even swindlers. The Swiss are frugal and solid and banking has been a part of their life for centuries. They are also artistic at meticulous craftwork such as the manufacturing of watches, clocks and the making of fine cutlery; but in the field of music and art they are unimaginative--you should go to a neighboring country if you wish to find these.

Along with the different languages, you may notice distinct architectural and cultural variations. For instance: Geneva, Lausanne, Montreux and Neuchatel reflect the French style, while Basel, Bern and Zurich are more German. These and other cultural differences, such as food variations, make this country truly interesting for the traveller.

The legend of William Tell, about whom everyone has heard (or has heard Rossini's opera about him) has been disproved as originating in

Switzerland.   Even   though   this   story depicts the character of the
Swiss,   the   legend comes from the Scandinavian region.   Nevertheless,
one   cannot   think of William Tell without thinking of Switzerland and
the legend will probably live on forever as a part of this country.

Switzerland is a popular and favored place to visit and no one will
regret a stay in this charming land.

The   dinner   hour   is usually at 7 o'clock and it is very important to
arrive   on time.   It is customary to bring flowers, or you may bring a
small   gift.   Any member of the family may greet you although it will
usually be the hostess. When you are visiting in the salon or living
room   there   may   be   no   beverages   served, or there may be some hors
d'oeuvres   and   Cinar   or   vermouth type drinks. After about one half
hour you will go to the dining room where the table will have a cloth,
although   in   some more modern homes there may be place mats and there
will   be   cloth   napkins.   Often the host will sit at one end of the
table and the guest of honor at the other.

Eating customs are about the same as in most areas of Europe. Wine is
drunk with the meal but no water nor coffee. There will be soup, meat
and   vegetables   and   salad, bread and dessert. Fondue is popular and
Raclette   is   served often, especially Zurcher Geschnetzeltes which is
white   veal,   and   Rosti   which is like hash brown potatoes. Rosti is
eaten   often   but usually not when there are guests. There are seldom
servants,   and   daughters often will assist their mothers in serving.
You   may   offer   to help but do not insist. The concentration of your
host   family   will   be   on making you comfortable and happy. Grace is
usually not said when there are guests. The guest begins to eat first
and   the   host   will tell you when to start. Coffee will be served in
the   living room after dinner and you should remain there for from one
hour to a maximum of about three hours.

You may send a thank you note the next day. Hotels in Switzerland are
some   of   the   best managed in the world and many students go there to
study the hotel business. However, a hotel is not considered by Swiss
people   to   be the best place to eat, therefore, if you wish to invite
your   hosts   to   a meal to reciprocate, try to find a small restaurant
with   some atmosphere. It is not necessary to call or to telephone to
say goodbye, but a card or letter a few months after returning to your
home will be appreciated. The Swiss like to
receive cards at Christmas.

Swiss Fondue

Grate 1/4 pound Gruyere cheese
1 clove garlic to rub the casserole for flavor (you can use a chafing
  dish)
2 teaspoons of potato flour
1 jigger of kirsch or dry sherry
1/2 cup white wine

12 pieces of toasted bread

After you rub the cooking utensil, throw the rest of the garlic away
and put the wine in. Cook for two minutes, then add the grated cheese
and bring to a boil while stirring. Mix the flour and sherry or kirsh
so that it is smooth in a little container and add this to the wine
mixture stirring all the time. This takes about three minutes and it
will become thick. Cut the toast into thin strips and serve it around
the hot dish. (You can keep a low flame under it if you have a dish
with a burner).   Each   person uses a long fork and dips the toast
pieces carefully into the center bowl until it is coated with the
sauce, then eats the fondue coated bread from the fork.

TAIWAN

Officially known as the Republic of
China, and also called Formosa, the
Island of Taiwan is a beautiful part of
the world. The island's capital is
Taipei. One of its mountains is 13,100
feet above sea level and parts of the
island are carefully cultivated. The
climate is semi-tropical and at times,
typhoons bring hard rains, winds and
floods. Most of the population is
decendent from the Fukien and Kwangtung
Provinces of mainland China who migrated
many years ago. Others migrated around
1950, with the collapse of Nationalist
China. The language is Mandarin Chinese
but may other dialects are also spoken. Japan ruled the area for a
number of years causing Japanese to be spoken widely. The religion is
mostly a combination of Buddhism and Taoism with some Christians.

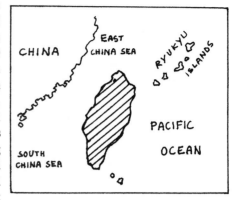

When invited for dinner, you should arrive on time and if you must be
late be sure to call your host and explain. You may arrive ten to
fifteen minutes early, but never late. You may bring a gift if you
wish, such as fruit, food, wine, canned food, candy or cookies, "a
little something for the children", but there is no need to bring
anything. Sometimes cloth yardage is brought to the hostess.

In a modern setting the living room will have chairs and a sofa. A
servant will probably greet you at the door and escort you to this
room. If the hosts are not yet in the room you should wait on a side
chair for them. Tea is served and sometimes cigarettes, cookies or
other sweets. You will visit for about one half hour and then enter
the dining room where tables may be round or square or oblong. There
will be chopsticks which are usually ivory, but may be bamboo and
sometimes silver, a decorated ceramic spoon and napkins. The seating
arrangement may be done in three ways:

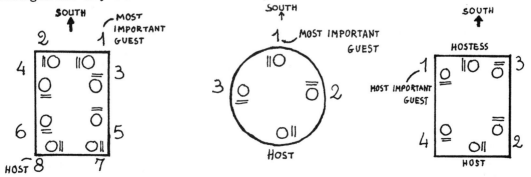

The chopsticks are placed on the table when one is not using them.
They should be put at the side of the bowl straight and parallel.
Often the dinner begins with a glass of whiskey or wine. "Gampey" is

the word for toast and the host will offer the first one. There will be taking during this interim and one must always drink when Gampey is said.

The actual meal may consist of sea foods, meat and vegetable dishes. The dessert may be cookies, other sweets or sometimes a sweet soup such as one made from dates. You may use the spoon for the soup or drink it from the bowl, leaving the spoon in the bowl if used. You may use your chopsticks to serve yourself by putting the food into your bowl. If there are nuts you should start with them first. You should sit in a straight position, not leaning over the table, near your bowl. To eat you may lift the bowl and hold it mid-chest high, not too close to your mouth. The whole meal may be on the table or it may be served separately. If the dinner is formal there may be no rice, otherwise you will be sure to have some. Should you spill anything, do not pick it up. You may, if you do not wish wine, tell your hosts that you prefer not to drink it and you will probably be offered a soft drink. Always say the food is good and try to eat some of everything. If the dinner has been prepared by your hostess she will be doubly happy when you praise the food. Sometimes meals are not prepared in the home but ordered and sent in from a store.
All will sit and talk for a long time when the meal is finished. Meals are to be enjoyed and the conversation should always be pleasant. The more traditional home will have a statue of Buddha on a stand in the center of the living room showing respect for the parents and there will be hard carved wooden chairs. One may be served tea and sweets. You should try to eat a little of each type of sweet offered to you. Here also the food may be complimented.

In the Republic of China there is a yellow wine called "Hawang jo" or Jo-Wine, which is about 20% alcohol. Sometimes liquor called "Kaoliung" is referred to as wine although it may be 90% proof. Rice wine is very popular and is also used for cooking.

When all have returned to the living room, tea is served again and one should remain for about one half hour, especially if the dinner has taken a long time. When your thank you hosts they may apologize for the food saying that it was not very good. You should argue with them and say that it was very good. Thank you notes are not sent and you will not be expected to call or write or to send a gift.

Always remember that with a Chinese dinner it is wise to eat small amounts at the beginning of the meal. You should find many diverse and interesting flavors and it will be difficult not to enjoy them.

Chinese cooking seems to be very complicated, but often it is quite easy to do. The main thing to remember is that frying is usually done quickly in very hot oil.

Sweet and Sour Fish

Take one good size fish for two to four people. Score the fish with many cuts and marinate it in a sauce of wine (white), ginger, onion juice and salt and pepper. After about one hour or less, coat the fish with cornstarch and egg yolk mixed. Now put some peanut oil in a shallow pan and get it very hot but be careful that it does not catch on fire. Put the whole fish in the pan. Keep the head resting in the pan as you lift the body to spoon over it the oil. Be sure it does not break, you have to be very gentle while spooning over it. After five or six minutes is long enough to cook it after it is all immersed in oil.

The quick cook sauce is made of oil as a base, then add a little tomato paste, vinegar, soy sauce, cornstarch, salt and sugar. You can judge the amounts you mix them and do what you think will taste best to you. Add to this one finely chopped onion, a green pepper which has been quartered and then cut up into small squares, and a little ground up garlic. A little bit of parsley for decoration, ginger and shredded onion mixed with some red pepper are added to the fish for eye appeal. Arrange the whole fish on a platter and pour any sauce over it, then add the decorative ingredients by sprinkling over the top.

This is a very popular dish and you can use the same ingredients to make sweet and sour pork. Cut the pork in little pieces after you have tenderized it by pounding with a meat cleaver and marinate it for about 1/2 hour. You may substitute pork oil for the peanut oil. Cover each piece of meat with the cornstarch mixture and vary seasoning by adding a little catsup.

TURKEY

Ankara, in north central Turkey, is the
capital. Here one can find fascinating
ruins which portray a varied history.
However, Ankara is not a "visitor's"
city such as Istanbul. Many Turks are
villagers who maintain their traditional
customs while others are completely
westernized. The weather varies from
one section of the country to another
going from mild to extremely cold
winters. Almost all the population is
Muslim and and most of these are Sunni
Muslim, but there is not declared
official religion. Turkish and Kurdish
are the main languages but English and

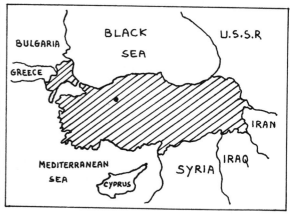

Arabic are also spoken. The country became a Republic in 1923 after
the downfall of the Ottoman Empire. Kemal Ataturk was the leader of
the new Turkey and he wished to modernize the country as swiftly as
possible. Records state that in order to make the people of his
country bow in subservience to no one, he insisted that the
traditional fez be replaced by a hat
with a brim. Thus the wearer could not
touch his forehead to the ground as the
brim would be in the way. A second
record states that Ataturk was once
hosting a state dinner of great
importance when suddenly one of the
servants slipped and spilled an entire
tray of food onto some of the guests.
Ataturk's remark, instead of a scolding,

was, "That shows you that the people of Turkey, who can do many
things, simply cannot make themselves into good servants!". The
history of Turkey is dramatic, sometimes cruel and always interesting.
The cuisine of turkey is one of the richest in the world. It became
important during the Ottoman Empire at which time the Topkapi palace
was built. The largest part of the palace is made up of kitchens.
Kushane-style food, which is even now a delicacy, derived its name
from small cooking pots known as kushane which translates to "bird
house". Ornate plates and cooking equipment were made of gold and
wrought copper.

There were special cooks or preparers for special dishes such as
sweets, yogurts, pastries, meat, poultry, fish, and vegetables, ice or
snow for cold beverages, etc. Pilaff, kababs, stuffed vegetables
known as dolma, and baklava were popular dishes.

Fish, which is abundant in Turkey, is steamed, grilled or fried, while
meat is usually in the form of a kabab on individual sticks. Lamb is
cooked on a large rotating spit and served with rice pilaff or cracked

wheat (bulgur). Baklava, a leaf pastry with layers of almond or walnut soaked in syrup or honey, is the most widely known Turkish sweet. Figs are internationally recognized as the finest.

The national strong beverage is raki, made of grape with anis seed flavoring. This is a refreshing but potent drink and should always be served with Turkish hors d'oeuvres. There are also excellent wines, beer and liquors. A non- drink which is very popular is cold watered down yogurt.

Dinner is usually eaten at about 7 o'clock and guests should arrive on time or up to ten minutes late. You may bring flowers or sweets if you wish. The hostess or daughter will probably greet you at the door and you will visit in the salon or living room for about one half hour. Sherry, vermouth and cognac may be served along with hors d'oeurves. Then the hostess or daughter will lead you to the dining room. The table is usually oblong and the host and hostess sit at opposite ends, the guests at the sides. There is usually a cloth, and napkins which sometimes may be paper. The silverware is of European style. There will be wine, water, soft drinks, bread and sometimes butter with individual small plates for it. The meal may consist of soup, meat such as steak or chicken (but no pork), rice or spaghetti, vegetables, some lima beans, dessert cakes which are heavy rich pastries, and tea and sometimes coffee. There will be little conversation and the servant, hostess or daughter will serve. You may hear the word for welcome to our home, "Hosgeldiniz", before you begin to eat. The host will begin to eat first and all follow immediately. At the end of the meal all return for about one hour to a maximum of three hours. Thank you is "Tesekur ederim". When you thank your hosts you should compliment the food.

It is not customary to send a thank you note or a gift or flowers. When leaving the country you may call or telephone and invite your hosts to visit you in your country. There is no need to write from home but of course you may do so if you wish.

In the more traditional setting dinner will be at about 5 o'clock. One should be on time and sweets may be brought to the hosts but no flowers nor gifts. The hostess will greet you and escort you directly to the family room where you will sit on pillows on the floor. Coffee will be served but no alcoholic beverages. You will eat in the same room at a low table. There will be a spoon for eating and fingers are used. All will eat from the center main dish and there will be no individual plates. Sometimes a prayer is said before the meal. Hands are washed in separate room before the meal and in that same room again after the meal. At the second washing you will be offered cologne to freshen your skin. If chicken is served you may be offered a damp napkin. Whereas the meat is cooked in an oven in the modern home, most villagers have no oven and it will be cooked more like a stew. The meat is always cut in small pieces. Conversation is sparse as this is not considered time to visit. You should leave rather soon after the meal and the coffee, as villagers usually retire early. The custom for thanking is the same as in the modern families.

UNION OF SOVIET SOCIALIST REPUBLICS

The USSR (Russia) is about two and one half times larger than the United States and its climate is much colder as most of the country is about 50° north latitude. Because of its size the weather varies and in the summer even Siberia is pleasant and warm in the more southern area. Here there are miles of forest and beautiful wild flowers and lillies on the lakes and ponds. In this part, there are many villages with log cabin homes. The log cabin method of building was first brought to the United States from Siberia. Along the railroad route the villagers prepare food which

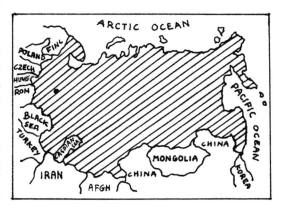

they sell hot to the passengers. This may be fried chicken, potatoes, piroshki, a bread with meat in it and other delicious snacks. There are about one hundred and seventy ethnic groups in Russia but most are Slav, Great Russians, Ukranians, Belorussians, Uzbeks, Tatars, Kazakhs, Azerbaydzhanis, Georgians, Lithuanians, Jews, Moldavians, Germans, Chuvashes, Tadzhiks, Poles, Mordva, Turkmens, Bashkirs, Kirgiz and Estonians each number more than one million in population. It is easy to see, therefore, that cultural habits differ throughout the nation. Foods and beverages also are traditional with each culture. The two main races to which all the people belong are European and Mongol and the blending of culture between the two occurs mostly in the larger cities.

Moscow is the capital of Russia and its people are ardent supporters of the ballet. The cities are clean and restaurants are plentiful. Since Russia became communistic atheism is considered to have displaced religions, although religions are still practiced by some of the people. Before the 1917 revolution, Russia was ruled by Tsars who inter-married with rulers of other countries and for this reason the aristocratic language of Moscow at one time was French. Russian is now the official language, and French spoken is rarely at this time.

The Indo-European family, which makes up the main part of the population, are linguistically categoried and include the East Slavs, Germans, Gypsies, Greeks, Iranians, Latvians, Lithuanians, Moldavians and Slavs. The second largest linguistic group is made up of Turkish speaking peoples, the Finns and Caucasians. Smaller groups are those made up of Mongols, Koreans, Chinese, Tungus, Ugrians, Paleo-Asiatics, and Semites. A large group which does not fit into the linguistic classification is that of the Jews.

A visitor to Russia can see a part of the population and believe that he or she understands the people, but it is obvious that knowing such a diversity of people can only be accomplished by living in the country for a long time one must remember that there is the mixture of cultures which has developed through the years which makes it even more confusing. But, as in all nations, there are threads which run through culture that may be quite similar. Russian music, for instance, may depict the differences, yet there will almost always be a strain which is unmistakenly that which we think of as "Russian".

Dinner is eaten at about 6 o'clock and if you are not a close friend, you will be invited for a specific time. A close friend will just be told to "come to dinner". You should arrive on time and it is customary to bring flowers or liquor; vodka or wine, if you wish. Any one in the family may greet you will visit in the living room where you will be offered something to drink and some hors de'oeuvres. Vodka is often drunk straight and is the best vodka in the world, not tasting strong as much of the vodka in other countries. Do not expect to be served caviar very often as most of it is exported and the supply has dwindled through the years. After about one half hour of talking you will go to the table which may be in part of the room or in a separate room. There will be a cloth, usually white with napkins and the standard silverware. Paper napkins are generally not used when guests are present. There will almost always be flowers on the table. Soup is popular but may not be served if it is a warm to hot summer evening. Wine and water will be available and bread, but no butter. Salad is eaten simultaneously with the meal which may consist of meat, rice, potatoes, vegetables, homemade cakes, ice cream or fruits. Food is passed at the table and it is considered polite to offer to help. You should compliment the food and you will probably sit at the table for a long time after the meal while conversation flows about all subjects. Russians are good conversationalists and they enjoy good food.

The word for a toast which all say is,"Nazdarovia". After you leave the table and return either to the sofa area or another room it is customary to remain from one half to about two hours. No thank you notes are sent but one may send flowers at anytime in Russia.

Borscht

Borscht is made in many ways, but two basic recipes follow:

2 cups shredded beets	1 tablespoon lemon juice
1 cup fresh tomatoes	1/4 cup sugar
4 cups water	4 eggs
1 small chopped onion	1/4 teaspoon salt
1/2 pound lean beef, cut into small pieces	Sour cream

Strain tomatoes over beets. Add water, onions and meat. Simmer about 30 minutes. Add lemon juice, sugar and salt. Boil for at least 30 minutes. Beat eggs, then add the hot borscht to them slowly while stirring carefully. Serve hot or cold with a teaspoon of sour cream dropped on each cup or bowl.

Borscht (with cabbage)

1/4 pound lean beef
1/2 pound pork
1 cup beets, chopped (the beets are
  not always included, as the soup is
  excellent with or without them)
1 large head white cabbage, chopped
  or sliced finely
1 tomato, quartered
1 large onion, sliced

5 or 6 cups water
2 teaspoons salt
1/4 teaspoon pepper
Dash of dill seed may be added
Sour cream

Put everything except the sour cream in a large cooking vessel. Cook
slowly a few hours until the meat is tender or soft. The meat is
often removed before serving depending upon the person's desire.
Serve hot or cold with a dot (about one teaspoon) of sour cream on
each bowl or cup.

THE UNITED STATES OF AMERICA

While a relatively new nation, the United States of America is old enough to have some established customs. In a country populated by so many diverse ethnic backgrounds one can understand the impossibility of explaining its traditions and culture in a few short sentences. Even its capital, Washington, D.C., was planned architecturally by a Frenchman. The native Indians, who themselves varied from section to section, have left their mark, the slaves who came to the South have left theirs and each immigrant, although coming to the "new world" to live a modern life,

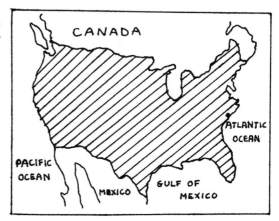

has brought native and often very ancient customs to influence the entire cultural make up of the country. To see how customs and times change one might read Common Sense in the Household by Marian Harland, by Charles Scribner's Sons, (1880). The 1907 edition is subtitled: A Manual of Practical Housewifery. This book was considered the "Bible" of cookbooks by many and it has some excellent recipes. It does not, however, consider various flavors or methods of cooking around the world and its recipes are quite provincial. But the most amusing part of the book pertains to servants who are carefully described, and also the method of "keeping them in their place" is even more carefully, if subtly, described. It seems a very foolish chapter in these times as servants are a true scarcity in the United States and when they do exist one can hardly recognize them as servants.

In the United States, wives and mothers often lead very busy lives and have little time to spend in the kitchen. This does not mean, however, that many are not superb cooks. In more recent years the interest in foods has changed drastically and many foreign recipes have been translated or blended to American preparation. The hamburger and "fast foods" are foods which you may buy at drive-in or easy stop restaurants and are increasingly popular. These are prepared quickly while you wait and may be served to eat at the restaurant or in your car. Potatoes are usually French fried and put into little paper bags, hamburgers are half-wrapped in paper in order to hold them while you eat. Beverages are usually milk shakes or soft bottled drinks. This kind of meal reveals Americans as a nation of people who are always "on the run" for they are consumed in a hurried lunch hour, on a work break, or while on a motor tour.

Cocktail parties are popular in American society. You may be invited for an intimate affair of just close friends, perhaps by a telephone call asking you to "drop by for cocktails". Usually the host will offer to mix you a cocktail and you should tell him what you wish to drink. You may order a glass of wine or sherry, or any type of drink you prefer. If you do not wish something with alcohol you may say so and ask for a soft drink or fruit or tomato juice. Large cocktail parties are usually by written invitation which will give the time, such as: "Cocktails from six to nine...". You may arrive anytime after six, although it is customary to be about one half hour late. You should leave no later than nine. Here there may be people serving a varity of cocktails and the hors d'oeuvres may consist of cheeses, small open sandwiches, olives,nuts, sausages, potato chips with a bowl of sauce to dip them into before eating, and other small helpings of foods to be eaten with fingers. Do not expect a full meal at this type of a party, although you may eat enough so that you will not wish dinner. It is wise to be cautious about the amount of cocktails you drink as they may be much stronger than they appear to be and, since the time will always be before the regular meal time, your capacity for alcoholic beverages may be less than you imagine. People who are new to these cocktail hours will also find that conversation may be difficult as guests tend to move around from friend to friend and have short conversations only. This is not a time for serious discussions. Most guests will stand as they talk and drink. Cocktail hours are very common during holiday seasons and some of the beverages, such as eggnog may be traditional for a specific holiday.

Picnics are another popular form of social gathering. A meal on the fourth of July (Independence Day) is often an outdoor picnic. Here, if the main course is meat, it is usually barbecued, or it may be the popular fried chicken. Paper plates and napkins are used and people help themselves from a variety of dishes such as baked beans, potato salad, corn, and desserts.

Barbecued foods are more widely served in the Western or South Western part of the United States because the weather is good and also the

Men have become interested in cooking and in some homes the may cook as much or more than the women. Always there is a plethora of pre-prepared and frozen foods, some of which are tasty and wholesome. From a country of "meat and potato" eaters, the United States has, for various reasons, including military involvements overseas, become a nation with many gourmets. The popular pizza, for instance, was brought from Anzio, Italy by the soldiers in the Second World War. Wines, especially those of California, rival the French, Italian, German, Chilean and others. Wine is now used in cooking, as a beverage at meals, and often in the place of the former strong cocktail before dinner. The turkey is a native bird to the American continent and is used extensively, especially for the traditional Thanksgiving meal. Corn-on-the-cob, southern fried chicken and barbecued meats are very popular in certain sections of the country.

In an American family the host and hostess will usually greet guests and escort them to the living room, or outdoor area if it is a barbeque, where a variety of cocktails may be offered accompanied by hors d'oeuvres. This visiting time may be from one half hour to more than one hour, depending upon when the guests arrive. It is polite to be prompt but some may arrive late. Dinner varies from home to home but usually will consist of salad, meat, vegetables, potatoes or rice. Often the meat will be supplanted with a casserole dish with or without meat in it. Fish and fowl are popular. Soup is not served as much as it is in European countries. Bread is always accompanied with butter and there will be small individual butter plates. The silverware is European style. Ice water will usually be on the table and a cloth or place mats may cover the table. Napkins may be cloth or, especially for barbecues, paper. Some families say Grace before eating. The hostess begins the meal by lifting her fork or spoon. Usually the dinner has an informal air and you may offer to help. In fact, men also may offer to help in the United States.

Catsup, or Ketchup, a thick tomato base sauce, is used extensively with these meals, not only for the meat but also for the French fried potatoes. It may surprise you to see someone dip the potatoes into this sauce before eating them. These meals tend to be starchy and seldom are accompanied by vegetables or fruits.

If you are visiting in a home and the hostess cooks the meals you may find that a part of, or all the ingredients are deep frozen and already prepared. These are simply heated until cooked according to the directions on each package. Sometimes a hostess will add spices or finish the preparations for certain dishes, but the main effort of cooking will have been done by the company which sells the product. As many women will have such a busy day that there is no time to cook a meal, these meals have become popular and the choice of dishes is extensive.

Whatever the food may be, you will find Americans very hospitable and comfortable to be with and you should enjoy your visit. Many times, if you offer to help your hostess with the dishes, all the guests may end up in the kitchen helping together. This, of course would be for a small and very informal group.

Desserts are every variety but mostly cakes, the famous apple or other pies, and ice creams. Fresh fruits are not eaten after dinner as often as they are in some European countries. Coffee, which is not very strong, is served either at table or in the living room after the meal. Here, one may be offered water, alcoholic beverages or soft drinks. It is customary to remain at least from one half to three quarters of an hour up to two or three hours depending upon the conversation and the family. Dicussion is continuous through the cocktail hour, the dinner and after the dinner.

When leaving you should thank the hosts and compliment the food if you wish. You may request a recipe if you especially like a certain dish. Always send a thank you note or call on the phone the following week. It is not customary to send flowers or a gift but you may do so if you wish. Your hosts will definitely wish to hear from you after you have returned to your country.

VENEZUELA

Caracas, the capital of Venezuela, is a city in a long valley high above the ocean where the airport is. The country's language is Spanish and the religions are Roman Catholic, Protestant and Jewish. The ethnic background of the population is Spanish, Portuguese, Italian, German and Native Indians. Venezuela was under Spanish rule almost since its discovery by Columbus until 1811. One of the earliest foreign students in the United States, at the time of Thomas Jefferson, was instrumental in forming the revolt that led to independence with Spain. In the

city of Caracas one finds old plazas and houses among the modern buildings.

When the Spaniards came to this area they found many Indian tribes, each having different dialects, customs, clothes and work habits. The Caribs, a war-like tribe, fought with the natives of some of the Caribbean Islands and had conquered some of the people living along the coast. The peace-loving Guajiros from the north still maintained their semi-primitive way of living. Those from the Andean highlands were more energetic and industrious. Diverse habits, even in the way in which they wove their cloth make it easy to distinguish one tribe from the other.

Most of the Indians, probably because they never banded together, finally were assimilated through conquest and colonialism. Their music, dances and ancient methods of weaving and making their ceramic objects, is about all that is left of them today.

Some natives say that you should arrive for dinner at the exact time for which you were invited while others say a Venezuelan is never on time, and always very casual or informal when he/she finally does arrive. There are two thoughts about this but you can probably be safer by arriving on time. You should arrive for dinner at the exact time for which you were invited and if you wish, you may bring wine, cookies, perfume, a book, a plant, flowers, or anything you think your hosts might enjoy. The host will probably greet you and escort you to the salon or living room for cocktails of wine, whiskey, beer, soft drinks, or home made "Meringada" with pineapple, papaya and mango. "Carati de mango" will be only mango juice. There may be hors d'oeuvres and often fruits cut in little pieces.

The dining tables are usually large and may have many dishes of food assembled on them. You may choose what you wish from these dishes and eat it when you wish during the meal. Salads may consist of boiled corn (large yellow), lettuce, cabbage, carrots, tomatoes and cucumbers with pre-mixed vinegar and oil dressing. There may be soup, meat, a paella, and sometimes baked potatoes and carrots. Desserts may be fruits and cheese and papaya al almibar.

One should say that he enjoys the food. At one time, it was thought best to have little conversation during meals but now all converse freely. At the end of the dinner, the host may stand and say how appreciative he is to have you as a guest and may discuss this relationship. Then the hostess may add some words and the guests then offer their appreciative remarks.

Hands are often washed before and after meals in a rest room nearby. When all return to the living room there may be tea, liquor and sometimes bon bons. Usually one remains for about one half to three quarters of an hour.

You may send flowers with a card of thanks and you should telephone to say goodbye. You may invite your hosts to your hotel or restaurant although this is not often done. A letter from your home after you have returned will be appreciated.

In villages, as in most countries, the people may be even more hospitable than in the large cities. The villagers will offer you more and more and they will love to see you eat their food.

Papaya Al Almibar

Green papaya, sliced, boiled and drained. Add sugar (papelon), vanilla and boil together until ready to serve as syrup.

YUGOSLAVIA

Yugoslavisa is a country where a visitor encounters many different kinds of interests and beauty. Belgrade, the capitol, is a city with a sense of business and busyness and it is nearby one of the loveliest natural areas of the country. There are lowlands, hills, acres of sunflowers, vineyards, a coastline, rugged mountains, islands, plains and diverse types of architecture from one area to another. The people have the most ethnic and religious diversity of Eastern Europe. The religions are Orthodox, Roman Catholic and Muslim and there are three 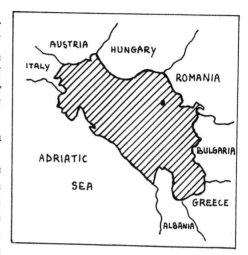 recognized languages: Slovenian, Macedonian and Serbo-Croation with others spoken in some areas. There has been much internal strife for many years and the country reflects the ethnic causes for these in its customs, costumes, foods and architecture. Rug making is famous although it is not of the same type as in Persia and India or China. The Romans left their mark, especially along the coast and on the small islands. Visitors may spend many interesting hours exploring this area which contrasts severely with that of the pastoral countryside of the interior. It is difficult to summarize Yugoslavian customs even though the people have been living in this part of the world for centuries. They are still too diverse.

You may bring your hosts a small gift, flowers, candy or wine and you should always arrive on time. In most every home the general European pattern of eating is acceptable. The host or hostess will probably greet you at the door and escort you to the salon or living room where all will visit for about one half hour or more. Maraschino liquor, Slivovich and different wines may be accompanied by hors d'oeuvres. Often Italian prosciutto and olives are used and hands are washed before the meal usually in a rest room. There will be a cloth and napkins and the usual silverware on the table. Water is often served to mix with the wine for those who wish to do so, but water is usually not served as a drink itself. However, if you wish some, it is possible to request it. There will be soup, a main course of meat and vegetables or one of the many stew like dishes which are delicious and popular, cheese with bread but seldom butter. For dessert there may be fruits, candy or cakes. The word for toasting someone's health is "Jivili". It is polite to praise the food. After dinner all return to the living room where Turkish coffee, cognac and other liquors may be offered. One should remain here for from about one half of an hour to one or one and a half hours.

Thank you is, "Hvala" and goodbye is "Dovidjenia". No note is sent to thank the hosts, but you may send flowers to the hostess. You may invite them to your hotel and you should write to them after you have returned from your travels.

The Yugoslavs are a hospitable people and they wish to make their guests happy and comfortable. They enjoy their foods and hope that others will enjoy them also.

Cevapcici

2 pounds of veal (white)
2 pounds of beef
1/4 pound of beef fat
4 teaspoons salt
2 teaspoons black pepper

Grind all these ingredients together until smooth. Then roll out into long sausage form and cut into pieces about two inches long each. Cook over a very hot fire (you can use charcoals) and roll them while cooking so they cook all through. Now chop two medium sized brown onions and serve them with the hot sausages.

Many dishes are very spiced and hot. There are a variety of stew like casserole dishes which differ in flavor depending upon the region where they are prepared. These are traditional dishes and you should attempt to find the dish of the region and taste each one if possible. Wines, beer and brandy are made locally and enhance the taste of these foods. With these, as with the prepared foods, it is wise to ask a local resident to suggest which beverage to enjoy with your specific meal.

INDEX TO FOOD AND BEVERAGES

INDEX TO FOOD AND BEVERAGES (Continued)